AUSTRALIAN

Language & Culture

Acknowledgments

Associate Publisher Mina Patria
Managing Editors Bruce Evans, Martine Power
Editors Janet Austin, Kate Mathews
Managing Layout Designer Chris Girdler
Layout Designer Carol Jackson
Production Support Larissa Frost, Chris Love
Product Development Janine Eberle, Laura Jane, David Kemp, Michael Ruff, Laura Stansfeld
Language Writers Denise Angelo, Peter Austin, Barry Blake, Susan Butler, Carolyn Coleman, Jane Curtain, Alan Dench, Mark Newbrook, Dana Ober, Paul Smitz, Jenny Tindale, Melanie Wilkinson
Maps Data supplied by the IAD Language Centre (p166, p170 and p173) and the Northern Territory Department of Education (p197)

Thanks

Sasha Baskett, Trent Paton, Piers Pickard, Kirsten Rawlings, Tony Wheeler

Published by Lonely Planet Publications Pty Ltd

ABN 36 005 607 983
4th Edition – March 2013
ISBN 978 1 74104 807 0
Text © Lonely Planet 2013

Cover Image Cover montage designed by Andy Lewis. Cover photographs: 270770, George Peters, Kolbz, Kwest Digital, Life on White, magnolianne, Pinch Creative, Robyn Mac, Silvrshootr, Yellow Garnet Photography/iStockphoto©

Printed in China   10 9 8 7 6

Contact lonelyplanet.com/contact

MIX
Paper from
responsible sources
FSC™ C021741

INDONESIA

PAPUA
NEW
GUINEA

EAST TIMOR

Arafura
Sea

Torres
Strait

Timor
Sea

Darwin

Arnhem
Land

Cape York
Peninsula

Great Barrier Reef

INDIAN
OCEAN

The
Kimberley

Gulf of
Carpentaria

Coral
Sea

Great
Sandy
Desert

NORTHERN
TERRITORY

Gibson
Desert

AUSTRALIA

Uluru

QUEENSLAND

WESTERN
AUSTRALIA

Pilbara

Simpson
Desert

Great Dividing Range

SOUTH
AUSTRALIA

Great
Victoria
Desert

Brisbane

NEW SOUTH
WALES

Nullarbor Plain

Flinders Ranges

Perth

Great
Australian
Bight

Adelaide

CANBERRA

Sydney

VICTORIA ACT

Tasman
Sea

Melbourne

SOUTHERN
OCEAN

Bass Strait

TASMANIA

Hobart

N 0   1000 km
0   500 miles

Look out for these...

CLASSIC PHRASE:
DIGGER

Miners ('diggers') on the goldfields always worked in pairs and came to symbolise mateship, via the soldiers of WWI

TRY THIS ONE:
COOEE!

An Aboriginal word yelled by bushwalking Aussies when they reach a particularly isolated area – to call their friends, or to hear the echo

USE WITH CAUTION:
SHEILA

Originally a word for any Irish woman, it became used for any woman (the female equivalent of 'bloke'), and a byword for ocker sexism

MISUNDERSTANDINGS:
KANGAROO

It does mean 'kangaroo', despite rumours that Aborigines had given Captain Cook the word for 'I don't know' (or something much ruder)

A SHORT HISTORY OF AUSTRALIAN

When the British government established a convict settlement in Sydney Cove in 1788 they wouldn't even have thought about the linguistic consequences. The history of Australian English is not just one of transplantation from the UK to Australia, within the dour confines of the First Fleet, but also of adaptation. As time went by, both the convicts and the free settlers adapted English to their new home, twisting the meanings of existing words and borrowing new ones to suit.

The beginnings of Aussie English

Convict influence

The earliest Australian English was very much a working-class variety, as the vast majority of the UK arrivals (mostly convicts) were poor and unskilled. Some words even filtered through from what was called the 'Flash Language' – the thieves' language of London – which earned an unexpected respectability on Australian shores. For example, in London 'plant' was the name for stolen goods hidden away to be collected later when it was safe. In early Australian English the word came to refer to stores and provisions hidden away in the bush to be collected on a return trip, and a matching verb 'to plant' was created. So when contemporary Australians speak of **planting** Christmas presents where the children can't find them, they're using old British criminal slang.

Early British influence

Words and expressions from British English took on a whole new meaning in colonial Australia. For example, in the UK a 'paddock' is a small enclosed meadow – in Australia a 'paddock' may extend further than the eye can see. In the UK a 'creek' is a small tidal inlet – in Australia a 'creek' is a subsidiary of a river and can be bigger than the Thames.

Australian English is predominantly a town-based language, as most of the convicts and early settlers were from British towns and cities, especially London and communities in the southeast of England. This partially explains why rural British English labels such as 'brook', 'glen' and 'dale' haven't become part of the Australian English vocabulary.

> ❝ DIGGER
> — A GOLD MINER; SYMBOL OF
> AUSSIE MATESHIP ❞

Early Irish influence

The other main influence on Australian English was Irish English, as convicts were also transported from Ireland following the 1798 Irish rebellion. Later on, in the 1840s, many Irish migrants were forced to settle in Australia after the potato famine. Australian English has therefore incorporated a number of Irish English words and phrases into its vocabulary. The term sheila, for example, is an Irish girls' name which was used in early Australian English to apply to any Irish girl, just as paddy was used for any Irish man. Later on sheila began to be used for any woman, although it's not a term women

BUSHRANGING

Bushranging is the robbery of settlers by thieves (**bushrangers**) who hide in the Australian bush. Ned Kelly (1855–80) is the most famous and iconic bushranger, and lives on in the Australian imagination as the personification of some prized characteristics: bravery, cheekiness and compassion for fellow battlers.

Ned led colonial authorities a merry dance for years, and his downfall only came about after he and his gang (which consisted mainly of his brothers) had held up the entire town of Glenrowan in Victoria. The Melbourne establishment sent out a trainload of police and trackers, but Ned organised **fettlers** (railway workers) to dig up the tracks and derail the train. Unfortunately for the gang, the Glenrowan schoolmaster escaped and managed to stop the train in time. The bushrangers donned homemade armour for the resultant shoot-out but were outnumbered, and only Ned survived to stand trial in Melbourne. His last words before he was hanged were said to be, 'Such is life'.

Other bushrangers worth a mention include Captain Moonlite and Captain Thunderbolt, who were good bushmen and rather elegant performers on the thievery stage. Brave Ben Hall was not so much a sinner as a man sinned against – he took to bushranging because of basic injustice. Mad Dog Morgan, on the other hand, was noted for his brutality.

have typically applied to themselves. In colloquial Australian English it also became a derogatory label for a man who was considered to 'behave like a woman', and is still wielded in this way by certain (sexist) Aussie males!

Irish English has also had some influence on Australian English grammar (see page 24).

Diggers & the goldfields

The gold fever that began afflicting prospectors in the 1850s led to an influx of people from all over the world, including the UK, Ireland, elsewhere in Europe, North America and Asia. Many British and American slang and colloquial expressions came to Australia during this period. Some words still survive from the diggings era – words like **fossick**, which used to mean 'dig through a heap of dirt for any leftover gold' and now means 'go carefully through anything in order to find something'. The word **digger** is another import from the gold rushes. It then referred to a miner, but since miners for safety reasons always worked in pairs, the digger became the symbol of mateship in Australia, particularly during the hardships of the World Wars.

20th-century Aussie English

The Federation of the Australian States, which was formed on 1 January 1901, was a watershed in Australian history and separates the former colonial society from the modern nation. Subsequently, there were a number of significant additions to Australian English.

> **LITTLE AUSSIE BATTLER**
> — A STRUGGLER WHO LACKS MONEY AND OTHER RESOURCES BUT BRAVELY BATTLES ON

FOOL'S GOLD

There's a story that **dinkum** (which means 'honest' or 'genuine', as do the expressions **fair dinkum** and **dinky-di**) is a Chinese word meaning 'real gold' and dates from the goldfields era, when distinguishing real gold from false was an issue, but this is apparently folklore. For a more popular etymology of dinkum, see p48.

In World War I, soldiers contributed some slang such as **furphy** (rumour). During the war, water was supplied to the soldiers in water carts made by John Furphy. The obvious place for the soldiers to exchange information of doubtful value was at the water cart, so these rumours came to be called **furphies**.

During the Great Depression the figure of the **battler** emerged (a person who struggles against all odds). The battler was usually surviving on the **susso** (sustenance payments). These days you'll often hear the rather simplistic phrase 'little Aussie battler' used to describe any Australian who lacks money and other resources but continues to slug it out with that ogre Life regardless.

World War II sparked an influx of Americanisms along with terms from army talk like **troppo** (madness from spending too much time in the tropics) and **spine-bashing** (resting).

Since the 1950s, Australia has received a significant number of migrants who speak a language other than English at home, including Italians, Greeks, Vietnamese, Chinese and Sudanese. Their English is often, of course, influenced by their other language, but there's not a lot of evidence that this has spread to the wider population.

Recent history

Australian English has been particularly influenced by American English over the last half-century. Although its English-speaking immigrants have mainly come from the UK, Australia's close ties with the USA and the worldwide influence of American music and movies have led to noticeable Americanisation. Australian kids appear to still use 'biscuit' rather than the American word 'cookie' and pronounce the letter z to rhyme with 'head' rather than with 'bee', but they readily refer to other people as 'guys' and 'chicks' and are apt to call good things 'awesome'.

As well as this Americanisation, Australian English is subject to the homogenising influence of nationwide television, movies and radio. Nevertheless, there are still differences between country and city speech, with country people tending to sound 'broader' and more colloquial.

Another noticeable pattern is the growing difference between the language used by older and younger generations. Much of the colloquial language that's regarded as distinctively Australian now tends to be used more by older people.

Aboriginal words

There aren't many words in Australian English that are borrowed from Aboriginal languages, but they often identify significant cultural items. The pattern of borrowing pretty much follows the precedent set by Captain Cook with **kangaroo** – words are only borrowed for totally new items. To European eyes the kangaroo was an extraordinary animal, quite unlike anything they'd ever come across before. Many other plants and animals could be named a native this or that – the koala, for example, was originally called a 'native bear' and the angophora was called the 'native apple' – but a kangaroo couldn't be thought of as a native anything. So, Cook asked the people of the Guugu Yimidhirr tribe of North Queensland what they called the animal, noted kangaroo in his diary, and thus the first major borrowing came about.

There's a curious sequel to this story. Relations between indigenous people and Europeans in Australia went from bad to worse, so that after the first great influx of Aboriginal words in the colonial period there was no traffic between Aboriginal languages and Australian English. So, when people finally became interested enough to attempt to track down the origin of kangaroo, they couldn't locate the word in local languages. They were possibly thrown off by the fact that whereas in English the difference between *k* and *g* is significant, in the language of the Guugu Yimidhirr there's no distinction between the two. In any case, a rumour developed that in fact Cook had been hoodwinked by the Aborigines and that the word kangaroo meant either 'I don't know' or something very rude. The misunderstanding has since been resolved – kangaroo means 'kangaroo' in anyone's language – but the folklore persists.

> **GONE tROPPO**
> — A MADNESS CAUSED BY SPENDING too MUCH tIME IN tHE HEAt AND HUMIDItY 'UP NORtH'

Billabongs & barramundi

The words that have been borrowed are generally the names of animals and plants. They come from a number of different Aboriginal languages, depending on where the Europeans turned up, with the largest number of borrowings coming from the languages of the east coast.

The Brisbane region

barramundi	fish
dilly	bag made of twisted grass or fibre
yakka	work

Inland New South Wales

billabong	waterhole
brigalow	tree
brolga	bird
budgerigar	small, brightly coloured bird
coolamon	wooden dish
gidgee	type of tree
quandong	type of tree with edible fruit
yarraman	horse

Inland Victoria

mallee	tree
mia-mia	rough shelter
mulga	type of wattle

HARD YAKKA

Yakka is a popular brand of work clothes worn by labourers, **sparkies** (electricians), **chippies** (carpenters), plumbers and other construction workers. It's obligatory to complete the outfit with a pair of **Blunnies** (Blundstone boots).

Northern Queensland

cooee	cry made to signal one's presence in the bush
kangaroo	kangaroo

The Outback

coolibah	species of tree
didgeridoo	long wooden musical wind instrument
nardoo	kind of fern

The Perth region

bardy	edible grub
euro	wallaby
jarrah	species of large eucalypt
karri	species of eucalypt
kylie	boomerang
marron	crayfish
quokka	small wallaby
wandoo	type of eucalypt
wongi	to talk

Southern South Australia

joey	baby kangaroo
willy-willy	sudden circling gust of wind
wurley	rough shelter

Southern Victoria

belah	tree
bingie	stomach or belly
yabba	talk

The Sydney region

bettong	rat-kangaroo
bogie	swimming hole
bombora	current over a submerged reef
boobook	small owl or mopoke
boomerang	curved piece of wood used as a missile
corella	large parrot, predominantly white with pink or orange-red markings
corroboree	Aboriginal ceremony
currawong	large black-and-white bird with yellow eyes and a loud ringing call
dingo	native dog
geebung	small tree
gibber	rock or stone
gunyah	rough shelter or dwelling
koala	'bearlike' marsupial
kurrajong	tree
myall	wild (from an Aboriginal word meaning 'stranger')
nulla-nulla	Aboriginal club or weapon
pademelon	wallaby
potoroo	small wallaby
wallaby	small cousin of the kangaroo
waratah	flower with large showy red petals, the emblem of NSW
warrigal	dingo
wombat	nocturnal marsupial the size of a small pig which lives in a burrow
woomera	Aboriginal weapon

MYTHICAL CREATURES

A small set of Aboriginal words are entrenched in the national folklore. What would the Australian dreamscape be without the **bunyip**, a mythical creature that lives in waterholes and is thought to cause loud noises at night and (rather more terrifyingly) devour women and children? The bunyip comes to us from Wemba Wemba, a language of western Victoria, and was described in the newspaper *Bell's Life in Sydney* as 'being about as big as a six months old calf, of dark brown colour, a long neck, a long pointed head, large ears, a thick mane of hair from the head down the neck, and two large tusks'.

Mythologically speaking, waterholes appear to be extremely dangerous places as they're also plagued by a hairy snake called the **mindi**. Watch out for the **yowie**, too, a huge ape-like monster from the stories of the Yuwaalaraay of northern New South Wales – the Aboriginal word translates as 'dream spirit'. On the plains of northern Queensland, you should also beware of the **min-min** light, a will-o'-the-wisp which is regarded as an evil apparition.

From Amaroo to Wagga Wagga

Aboriginal words and their meanings were also appropriated for Australian English place names, including the following:

Allora	waterhole; a town in Queensland
Amaroo	beautiful place, red mud or rain; a town in New South Wales
Babinda	waterfall; a town in Queensland
Dandenong	lofty mountain; a mountain range in Victoria
Dorrigo	stringybark; a town in New South Wales

Dunedoo	swan; a town in New South Wales
Ekibin	a part of the river where indigenous people could obtain edible aquatic roots; a place in Brisbane
Murrumbidgee	big water; a river in New South Wales
Narooma	blue water; a town in New South Wales
Ulladulla	safe harbour; a coastal town in New South Wales
Wagga Wagga	crows; a town in New South Wales (pronounced 'wogga wogga' – most Australians just call it plain 'wogga')
Waikerie	wings or anything that flies; a town in South Australia

❝ COOEE
— CRY MADE to SIGNAL ONE'S
PRESENCE IN tHE BUSH **❞**

In the 1990s, after decades of no borrowings, some new Aboriginal words began to be added to Australian English. A notable one is **Koori**, a word from the Awakabal tribe near Newcastle, just north of Sydney. Koori has been used by some Aborigines to refer to an Aborigine of eastern Australia since the early part of last century.

Place names have also started being borrowed again, beginning with the reinstatement of the Loritdja word for that great red monolith in central Australia, **Uluru** (formerly known as Ayers Rock). Similarly, the nearby Olgas are now once again **Kata Tjuta** and Kings Canyon is **Watarrka**.

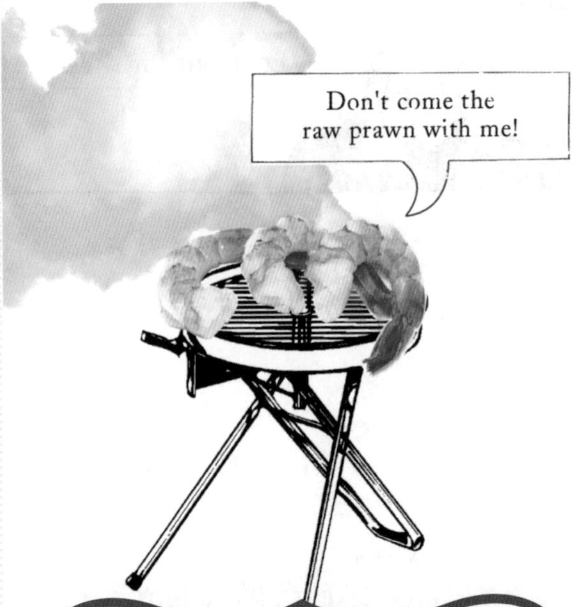

SPEAKING AUSTRALIAN ENGLISH

Look out for these...

CLASSIC PHRASE:

YOU LITTLE RIPPER!

Not much used these days, it's a classic Australian way to express a positive opinion

TRY THIS ONE:

NO WORRIES

It's said to sum up the laid-back and agreeable Australian attitude

USE WITH CAUTION:

DAZZA'S DRINKING BUNDY AT THE BARBIE WITH A MUSO DOWN FROM BRIZZIE

Australians love shortening their words but the endings can be unpredictable

MISUNDERSTANDINGS:

BASTARD

It's not always an insult and in some circumstances can be used with compassion or even affection

SPEAKING AUSTRALIAN ENGLISH

Being informal and speaking informally is an important part of Australian culture, and slang and colloquial language are a normal part of Australian English – though of course Australians can be as formal as anyone else when it's appropriate. It's thought this informality is partly due to the fact that most of the first English-speaking settlers in Australia were convicted criminals. In any case, for many Australians being informal expresses desired values of equality and solidarity. Australians often portray their country as classless, and while this is not entirely true, it's certainly a lot less class-conscious than, say, the UK.

Barbaric noises

Very early in the days of colonial settlement, British visitors were prone to commenting (usually disparagingly) on the Australian accent. Various attempts were made to correct the 'twisted vowels' and 'barbaric noises' made by the locals from that early point in colonial history until comparatively recently. But the accent that formed among the descendants of the convicts and settlers has proven remarkably resistant to such efforts. There are two main theories on how the Aussie twang came about – the 'melting pot' theory and the 'stranded dialect' theory.

The melting pot theory

The early convict settlements included speakers of various British dialects, whose accents remained much as they were before they landed on Australian shores. Being transported didn't change a

Yorkshireman into something else, and there was no way that Cockney convicts were going to start imitating their military masters. But the children of the convicts were like children anywhere – eager to conform and win the acceptance of the other children. So, the theory is that with no one particular local form of language to guide them, they forged a new accent of their own by blending the various accents represented among them.

> **❝ BOOBY ISLAND, BUTTY HEAD, BANANA, HUMPTY DOO**
> **— STRANGE PLACE NAMES ❞**

The stranded dialect theory

The melting pot theory does seem to have a lot going for it, but there's an alternative – that there was a predominant dialect among the convict community which became the Australian English of today, but that this dialect is difficult to trace back to its British origins for two reasons. Firstly, although there's a conservative force operating in a colony that resists change, that force doesn't operate back in the mother country, where the dialect continues to change. So, the older form is stranded in the colony.

Secondly, circumstances may have forced changes on the colonial speakers which confused the issue, making it harder to decide just what the original home accent was. The presence of a large group of speakers with one accent, for example, might bring about changes in the speech of the rest of the community simply through the pressure of numbers.

We can't know for sure which (if any) of the theories is right. Perhaps both are partly valid.

The influence of US pronunciation

Although American English has had an obvious influence on Australian vocabulary (and on some areas of grammar), very few words show any American influence on their pronunciation. It's said that the only time Australians actually sound American is when they're crooning popular songs – a vocal crutch shared by pop singers from other English-speaking communities. However, this too may be changing, as more Australian musicians seem to be singing in their normal accents.

Differences across Australia

Australian English is remarkably homogeneous, despite the fact that it's over 3000km from the west coast to the east. Most speakers sound the same or very similar, and there are no big regional differences compared to the UK or the USA. The main geographical difference is thought to be the city versus country divide – the rural accent is supposedly slower and broader than the urban.

Still, there is some evidence that subtle differences in pronunciation between regions do exist. For example, many people in Melbourne, Brisbane and Hobart use the short *a* vowel (as in 'cat') in words like 'castle', 'graph' and 'dance', while the long *a* (as in 'cart') is normally used in other parts of Australia. Similarly, in South Australia and parts of Victoria the word 'school' and others like it tend to be pronounced with a clipped, shortened vowel not common elsewhere. Some linguists believe these sorts of changes are becoming more noticeable. (For more on differences in speech across Australia, see page 133.)

One distinctive pattern that has emerged among young people over the past few decades is the use of the high rising terminal, or 'uptalk' – statements like 'That's my favourite film' have the rising pitch which is usually reserved for questions. Australian soap operas popular in the UK have been blamed for infecting British speech with rising intonation; it's ridiculed there as 'Australian Question Intonation'.

Grammar

There aren't many grammatical features exclusive to Australian English, but the ones that exist can sometimes cause a little confusion for visitors.

all/both ... not   when Australians say things like 'All those letters didn't arrive', they usually mean 'None of those letters arrived'. Older Australians don't often use such sentences, but if they do they put the stress on 'all' and the sentence then means 'Some of them arrived and some didn't'. Just to add a bit of excitement to the day, some people use both meanings.

as such   Australians sometimes use 'as such' in cases where 'so', 'therefore', or a similar expression would be usual elsewhere: 'The building's locked; as such, we can't get our things'.

as well   like Canadians (but not like most Americans or British), Australians sometimes begin sentences with 'As well' as in 'As well, there are three other problems'.

conditionals   in Australia, the phrase 'If that happened...' doesn't always mean that the speaker thinks the event in question might happen (but probably won't) in the future, as in 'If that happened tomorrow I'd be surprised'. It sometimes means that it *could* have happened in the past but didn't, as in 'If that happened yesterday I'd have been surprised'. Most people from other English-speaking countries would say 'If that had happened...' or, in the USA, 'If that would have happened...'

different to   the majority of Australians use 'to' after 'different', as in 'Adelaide is very different to Perth'. Some older people and most formal writings still use the more typically British word 'from'. However, the originally American form, 'different than', is becoming increasingly popular.

BATMANIA

Rumour has it that Melbourne narrowly escaped being named 'Batmania' in honour of John Batman, who selected the city's site in 1835. But even without 'Batmania', Australia still has its fair share of places with strange names. Some intriguing ones include:

Bald Head (WA)	Indented Head (Vic)
Banana (Qld)	Lake Disappointment (WA)
Big Billy Bore (Vic)	Mexican Hat Beach (WA)
Booby Island (Qld)	Mt Hopeless (SA)
Broken Bucket Reserve (Vic)	Nightcap (NSW)
Butty Head (WA)	One Arm Point (Vic)
Cape Liptrap (Vic)	Salmon Gums (WA)
Humpty Doo (NT)	Snug (Tas)

hottest, highest, etc   when an Australian news report says that yesterday was the hottest May day since 1927, it doesn't imply – as it might elsewhere – that the day in May 1927 was even hotter, it implies that it was the same temperature. This can be very confusing at first for people addicted to weather or statistic-laden sport reports.

irregardless   this word is a blend of 'irrespective' and 'regardless' and has the same meaning ('Irregardless of what you think, I'm going to do it!'). It's heard elsewhere but seems to be especially common in Australia.

may & might   if an Australian says something like 'Bruce may have sung', sometimes the singing referred to *could* have happened but didn't. Most non-Australians would use 'might', not 'may', in this case. Using 'may' would normally mean that they don't know whether it happened or not. Australians also often say things like 'Pete said that Bruce 'may sing', even where the singing predicted by Pete would be in the past if it had happened. Again, 'might' would be more usual elsewhere.

mustn't as in Ireland and parts of England, Australian English uses the word 'mustn't'. Many Australians say things like 'She mustn't be in – the lights are all out'. In most other English-speaking countries people would say 'She can't be in' or, in the USA, 'She must not be in'.

my same some Australians say things like 'Can I keep my same phone number if I change address?' In the majority of other English-speaking countries the expression in such cases is always 'the same'.

usedn't to for most English speakers, the negative of 'used to' is 'didn't use to', as in 'I didn't use to like beer but now I do'. The older form 'usedn't to' ('I usedn't to like beer...') is now rare, but Australia is one of its remaining habitats.

❝ KIDDIEWINKS

— CHILDREN ❞

verbs used with team names in Australia, as in America, the names of sports teams can be either singular or plural. So people may say either 'West Coast (the football team) is doing well' or 'West Coast are doing well'. In the UK, by contrast, team names are always plural ('Liverpool are doing well'). Although it's less common, Australians also use singular nouns and pronouns to refer to teams occasionally. So in an Australian newspaper, a sentence like 'It's the reigning champion' could refer to a football team.

youse pronounced 'yooz', this has become the plural of 'you'. You may hear sentences like 'Where are youse going?' Only used by the grammatically challenged.

Shortened forms

Australians are fond of cutting their words down to size, usually by taking the first part of the word and finishing it off with *-ie* or *-o*. This can be used to indicate affection, especially on names but also on ordinary words – children, for example, are sometimes referred to as **kiddies,** or even more playfully, **kiddiewinks** (thereby considerably extending the length of the original word, but increasing the affection). The *-ie* ending is also used to create useful new nouns from adjectives – like the word **greenie** (person concerned about the environment) from green. The *-o* ending is a bit more neutral than the *-ie* one and can be used to convey a certain nonchalance.

There's a school of thought that says the Australian addiction to abbreviation, with all its informality, is due to a middle-class desire to appear down to earth despite craving an upper-class standard of living – in other words, people want to live like the elite but can't stand to think of themselves as elitist.

Note that it's not unusual to find words ending in *-ie* also spelled with a *-y* ending. Thus **cabbie** could well be spelled **cabby.** However, for some inscrutable reason various words always take *-ie* and others always take *-y*. In the same way, some words can take *-o* as well as *-ie* or *-y*, but some only take *-o*. Here are some of the more common *-ie* words:

Aussie	Australian
barbie	barbecue
bickie	biscuit – 'big bickies' means a lot of money
bikie	motorbike rider
Blunnies	Blundstone workboots
bookie	bookmaker at sporting events
brekkie	breakfast
brickie	bricklayer

Brizzie	Brisbane
cabbie	cab/taxi driver
cardie	cardigan
chippie	carpenter
chockie	chocolate
Chrissie	Christmas
ciggie	cigarette
conchie	conscientious person, or conscientious objector
druggie	drug addict
flattie	flathead (fish), or flat tyre
foodie	a gourmet
freebie	something for free
goalie	goalkeeper
goodies	treats
hottie	hot-water bottle
jarmies	pyjamas
leckie	electric blanket (or, for twice the impact, **leckie blankie**)
lippie	lipstick
littlie	little thing, or child
meanie	mean person
newie	new item
oldie	old item, or your parents (when in the plural)
pokie	poker machine
pollie	politician
possie	position (pronounced 'pozzie')
postie	mail deliverer

prezzie	present
prozzie	prostitute
rellie	a relative
rollie	'roll-your-own' cigarette
sickie	day off sick (or supposedly sick)
sparkie	electrician
subbie	subcontractor
sunnies	sunglasses
swiftie	a trick – **to pull a swiftie** is to trick someone
taddie	tadpole
Tassie	Tasmania (pronounced 'tazzie')
tinnie	can of beer
trannie	transistor radio, or transvestite

YEAH NAH

In the past, if an Australian paused or hesitated before answering a question asked, they'd often fill the gap with an 'um' – in the case of the more ponderous talker, extended to the length of a monk's meditative chant. But nowadays the humble 'um' seems to have yielded to the contradictory, self-cancelling and terribly addictive 'yeah no' (or more typically, 'yeah nah'). It's common, for instance, to hear media interviewees (particularly sportspeople) begin their answer to a journalist's question with a firm 'yeah nah'. Some linguists believe that 'yeah no' acts as more than just a gap-filler, and is a way of politely accepting and then downplaying or questioning a compliment or assertion.

truckie	truck driver
U-ie	U-turn in a car (pronounced 'yoowee')
umpie	umpire
undies	underpants
wharfie	a wharf labourer
Windies	the West Indian cricket team
Woolies	Woolworths (supermarket chain)
woollies	woollen clothes

A few words that nearly always use the -*y* spelling include:

Bundy	Bundaberg rum, or Bundaberg (a town)
comfy	comfortable
divvy van	police divisional van
dunny	toilet
exy	expensive
footy	football
kindy	kindergarten
placky	plastic
Rocky	Rockhampton
stubby	bottle of beer
telly	TV

BAZZA HEARD A SHEILA SAY...

According to *The Story of English* (Penguin Books, 1986), well-known Aussie performer Barry Humphries claimed he once heard an Australian woman describing her hospital visit for a hysterectomy as 'having a **hizzie** in the **hozzie**'.

The following always take -o:

ammo	ammunition
arvo	afternoon
avo	avocado
combo	combination
compo	compensation
demo	demonstration
dero	derelict person
doco	documentary
Freo	Fremantle
garbo	garbage collector

> **GET YOUR WOOLLIES FROM WOOLIES**
> — GET YOUR WOOLLEN CLOTHES FROM WOOLWORTHS SUPERMARKET

gyno	gynaecologist
info	information
intro	introduction
journo	journalist
kero	kerosene
metho	methylated spirits
milko	milk deliverer
muso	musician

porno	pornography, or pornographic
rego	car registration
Salvo	Salvation Army member
servo	petrol station
smoko	break for a cigarette
speedo	speedometer
vego	vegetarian person or meal (pronounced 'vejo')
wino	an alcoholic who drinks cheap wine

Warnie, Kyles & Bazza

Nicknames are all but compulsory in Australia and only rarely will a person be called by their given name (especially on the sporting field). The most common nicknames are affectionate shortenings of first names or surnames to end in *-ie*, *-o* or *-y*. Rules apply: John (or Mr Johnston) is always Johnno, Matthew is always Matty. Some names, such as Lachlan, go either way – both Lacho and Lachie are permitted. Oddly, some other names that already end in an *-ie* sound (like 'Kylie') are often transformed into something else again ('Kyles' in this case).

The ending *-zza* is also popular, hence the following:

Barry	**Bazza**
Darren	**Dazza**
Gary	**Gazza**
Karen	**Kazza**
Kerry	**Kezza**
Murray	**Muzza**
Sharon	**Shazza**
Terry	**Tezza**

CHOOKS, CROCS & COCKIES

Given their penchant for shortening existing words and inventing new ones, it'll come as no surprise that Australians have given their friends (and foes) in the animal world a few 'special' names:

barra	barramundi (fish)
bitie	biting insect
blowie	blowfly
bluey	blue heeler dog
boomer	large kangaroo
brumby	wild horse
budgie	budgerigar
bug	small crustacean, as in 'Moreton Bay bug'
bushman's clock	kookaburra
chook	chicken
cocky	cockatoo, or cockroach
croc	crocodile
dunny budgie	fly
freshie	freshwater crocodile
maggie	magpie
mozzie	mosquito
muddie	mud crab
roo	kangaroo
saltie	saltwater crocodile
sandie	sand crab
stinger	stinging jellyfish, especially box jellyfish
yabby	small freshwater crayfish

G'day, hooroo

G'day is the most famous Australian greeting, so it might surprise you to learn that plain old **Hi** is often much more common, particularly in the cities. Here are some others:

Hey

Hiya

How are ya?

How's it going?

How ya goin' mate – orright? (older generation, often male)

How's tricks?

> ❝ CHECK YA
> — GOODBYE ❞

Note that the correct response to any of these questions (as in other English-speaking countries) is almost always 'Good, thanks'.

The handshake is the most widely accepted form of physical contact between strangers or acquaintances when greeting. Hugging and cheek kissing are common between friends and relatives for both greetings and goodbyes, but not between strangers. Of course, this rule is thrown completely out the window when enough alcohol is involved!

Here are a few verbal farewells:

Catch you (later)

Check ya later (or just **check ya**)

Ciao

Hooroo! (old-fashioned)

See ya (later)

Drought & flooding rains

Conversations about the weather in Australia are rarely limited to talk of sunshine or rain. Some parts of the country are subject to unique weather patterns and climatic events that have acquired their own terminology. The country's far north, for example, has two distinct seasons: **the Wet** (roughly November to April) and **the Dry** (May to October). The build-up to the wet season, which takes place during October and into November, can be a hellishly uncomfortable time for locals and visitors alike – temperatures rise, the humidity soars and people tend to go a bit nuts. For this reason, this interim period is also called the **troppo season** or **mango madness** (mangoes are harvested around Darwin and Katherine at this time).

The Tiwi Islands, off the coast of the Northern Territory, have personalised the afternoon thunderstorm that lashes them almost daily during the build-up to the Wet – they call it **Hector**. The type of violent thunderstorm that occurs in the Top End at the end of the Wet is called a **knock 'em down storm**, because it flattens the spear grass that has grown high during the rainy season. In Tasmania, significant rainfall can occur year-round, particularly in the west of the island, which may explain why the locals sometimes refer to rain optimistically as **liquid sunshine**.

> ❝ MANGO MADNESS
> — THE CRAZY-INDUCING BUILD-UP TO
> THE WET SEASON IN THE FAR NORTH ❞

The **Fremantle doctor** is a Western Australian phenomenon – an afternoon sea breeze that cools both Perth and the Western Australian town it's named after. Other Western Australian towns have their own versions of this breeze, hence you might

SPEAKING AUSTRALIAN ENGLISH

hear references to the Esperance doctor or the Albany doctor, which reaches inland all the way to Kalgoorlie.

Far north Queensland experiences something less pleasant: **the big Bedourie**, which is a large dust storm.

....

No worries!

Australians are known for their easygoing nature and friendliness, and have few hard and fast rules about social behaviour. **No worries** is a popular Australian response akin to 'no problems', 'that's OK' or 'sure thing'. There is one exception, however: if you have negative opinions about local places, try to be low-key about it. Though outwardly imperturbable, some Australians will be offended – the older generation in particular can be prone to **cultural cringe** (feeling that one's culture is inferior to that of other countries). Positive opinions, of course, can be easily expressed with true-blue words like **beaut**, **bewdy**, **bonzer** or **ripper**.

For details of the etiquette when it comes to that great Aussie tradition, the pub shout, see p81.

A NATION OF BASTARDS

In Australia, the word **bastard** has an extremely varied job description and it rarely (if ever) refers to illegitimacy. Sometimes it's used in an affectionate way – 'G'day, you old bastard!' – or compassionately – 'Poor bastard lost his job'. But it's just as likely to form part of a string of abusive terms during a fiery exchange, or to be used to describe something annoying ('I can't fix this bastard of a thing!') or someone vile – 'He's a mean bastard'. To confuse you even more, it's also sometimes used to describe *any*one, as in 'Should that bastard be fishing there?'

❝ BEAUt, BEWDY, BONZER, RIPPER

— GOOD ❞

A bit of a barney

Among themselves, Australians can make comments that sound to the untrained ear like abuse, but in reality are often mild, good-humoured digs. Australians have a well-stocked arsenal of useful, socially acceptable insults that can be flung at someone else as long as the basic intention is amiable; accompanying them with a reassuring smile doesn't hurt either. Here are a few, all of which basically mean 'idiot':

bloody drongo   a drongo was a horse that came second in all its races

boofhead   possibly derived from the 16th-century word for a fool, 'buffle', which was a borrowed French term of abuse (in French it means 'buffalo')

dumbcluck   referring to the proverbial idiocy of chickens

(you great) galah   a galah is a type of bird that has a reputation in Australia for being noisy, gregarious and stupid

nincompoop   someone has suggested that this is a mispronounced version of the Latin phrase 'non compos mentis' meaning 'without control over your own mind', but no one really knows for sure

When a relatively polite, friendly argument takes a serious turn and the participants end up having **a bit of a barney** (an

BRICKIE'S CLEAVAGE

A **brickie's cleavage** is the flash of buttock cleft exposed by excessively low-riding trousers or shorts. This cheeky look was once confined to labourers who couldn't bear to part with worn-out workwear, but fashionable low-slung jeans have led to an explosion of brickie's cleavage amongst the general population.

Other ear-catching body-part terms include:

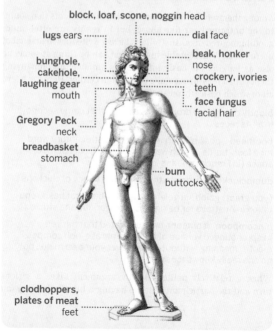

block, loaf, scone, noggin head

lugs ears

dial face

beak, honker nose

bunghole, cakehole, laughing gear mouth

crockery, ivories teeth

face fungus facial hair

Gregory Peck neck

breadbasket stomach

bum buttocks

clodhoppers, plates of meat feet

old-fashioned phrase meaning an argument), you may hear one or more of the following terms used to describe it:

argument   bust-up; (wing-)ding; set-to

fight   argy-bargy; barney; blue; box-on; bust-up; donny-brook; dust-up; free-for-all; go-in; punch-up; rough-house; run-in; set-to; yike

The people involved might be described as:

angry   aggro; fit to be tied; foaming at the mouth; hot under the collar; ropeable

crazy   a basketcase; has a few roos loose in the top paddock; lame-brained; the lift doesn't go to the top floor; not the full quid; silly as a two-bob watch; troppo; a wacker

cross with someone   dark on someone; dirty on someone; miffed; narked on someone; narky; shirty; snakey; sore

in a bad mood   browned off; cheesed off; fed up to the back teeth; has the shits; pissed off; snitchy; ticked off; uptight

> **BLOODY DRONGO, BOOFHEAD, GREAT GALAH**
>
> — YOU IDIOT

Or they might be called names like:

coward   a damp squib; dingo; a gutless wonder; nervous Nellie; piker; scaredy-cat; sook; wimp; wuss; yellow-belly;

idiot   alf; dickhead; goose; imbo (short for 'imbecile'); mug alec; nong; wombat

During the fight, some of the following things might happen:

to abuse   bore it up someone; get stuck into someone; give someone a blast; give someone heaps; tip the bucket on someone

to be in trouble   be in more strife than Ned Kelly; up shit creek

> ❝ GET A BIG BLACK DOG UP YA!
> — GET lost! ❞

to fight   bash up; come to blows; go the knuckle; mix it with someone; stack on a turn

to get scared   chicken out; go to water; pack death; pack shit; pike out; take a willy

to lose your temper   blow a fuse; blow your stack/top; chuck a mental; chuck a wobbly; crack the shits; cut up rough; do your block/nana; flip your lid; get off your bike; go bonkers; go nuts; go off your brain; go through the roof; lose your cool; spit chips; spit the dummy

to tease   chiack; razz someone; rib someone; send someone up; stir; take the mickey out of someone

And of course one of the participants might be told to:

Get lost!   Bite ya bum!; Get a big black dog up ya!; Get a rat up ya!; Get knotted!; Get stuffed!; Rack off (hairy legs)!

Look out for these...

CLASSIC PHRASE:
FAIR DINKUM

Meaning honest or genuine, this is a fair dinkum Aussie saying

TRY THIS ONE:
CLICK

Because 'kilometre' is such a long word

USE WITH CAUTION:
DUNNY, CRAPPER, THUNDERBOX

There are numerous names for the toilet – choose the appropriate one based on the company you're in

MISUNDERSTANDINGS:
SPUNK

Do not be alarmed! In Australia this word means a good-looking person

LIVING LIFE – THE AUSSIE WAY

Tourist campaigns over the years have sold Australia as a land of fit, fun-loving (read 'boozy'), laconic, relatively carefree and above all resilient people, perpetually at play, competitive to the last and never short of a tall story. As with all stereotypes, there's some truth in this. But the collective Australian identity is forged from much more than beer, sport and irony.

Bullamakanka versus the big smoke

The basic division, physically and culturally, for many Australians is between the country (the bush) and the city. Although most Australians live in the cities – which are all, with the exception of Canberra, on the coast – they tend to romanticise the bush and see it as iconically Australian – its flora and fauna, its vast deserts, mountain ranges, rivers and plains.

The country

A number of terms have been created to express the vastness and mythical quality of the landscapes in the country's interior. The best-known example is **the Outback**, a catch-all name for the remote Australian interior. Here are some others:

back of Bourke   an unspecified area which is beyond Bourke, a remote town in northwestern New South Wales, on the fringe of the outback. Shorthand for any remote area. **Bullamakanka** and **Woop-Woop** are probably **back of Bourke**.

beyond the black stump   there are a million pubs and motels in New South Wales which claim to have the authentic black stump that explorers went beyond. The phrase most likely came from the practice of giving directions in remote areas based on landmarks like strange-shaped rocks, hills and, of course, the ubiquitous blackened stump.

Bullamakanka   an imaginary remote town which has a pseudo-Aboriginal name and is totally **hicksville**; also called **Woop-Woop** or **Bandywallop**

the Never-Never   this term refers to areas of Queensland and the Northern Territory. There's a theory that the word is an anglicisation of an Aboriginal name for these regions, **Nivah Nivah**. Whatever the truth, the English version conjures up the ultimate state of being lost and forgotten. Jeannie Gunn used this term in the title of her classic 1908 novel about Top End life, *We of the Never-Never*.

Many Australian country people live on farms or properties – in the more remote areas, often on huge stations (roughly equivalent to 'ranches' in America), which can be bigger than whole European countries. There are a number of distinctively Australian figures populating the farming stratosphere, including:

cocky farmers   small landholders, so called because they are said to resemble the cockatoo that scratches in the dirt to find food. They come in various flavours: **cane cockies** (sugarcane farmers), **cow cockies** (dairy farmers) and **wheat cockies** (wheat farmers).

graziers   station-owners who run sheep or cattle. The grazier is likely to be part of the **bunyip aristocracy** or **squattocracy**, the crème de la crème of country society.

jackeroo/jillaroo   a jackeroo or jillaroo is a young man or woman who works at a station doing various jobs to gain experience

rouseabout   a stationhand who's expected to do all the odd jobs. In the shearing shed it's the rouseabout who rushes up with tar for a cut sheep and takes the fleeces to the sorting table.

A TOWN LIKE ALICE

The Alice is what locals call the town of Alice Springs in the Northern Territory, which lies roughly in the centre of Australia. Alice Springs was named after Alice Todd, wife of the man responsible for the construction of the Overland Telegraph Line completed in 1872, which connected Darwin to Adelaide.

Other country folk include the following:

boundary rider   the boundary rider patrols and maintains the fences encircling the vast acreage of an outback station, as well as the incredibly long fences erected by state governments for various reasons (to keep rabbits from crossing into Western Australia or to keep dingoes out of settled New South Wales). Such riders often don't see another human being for months on end, so naturally there's a tradition that they are loners who are happy to be by themselves in the bush.

bushie   a **bushman** or bushie is someone who lives capably in the bush. The legend of the bushman is that he's totally at home in the bush and knows all its ways – never gets lost and can always find food and water – and he's usually on good terms with the local Aboriginal people, from whom he's learned a thing or two.

swagman   the swagman or **swaggie** is a tramp. He carries his swag **on the wallaby track** (shortened to 'on the wallaby') and is often a good bushman too. A **sundowner** is a type of swaggie who times his arrival at a station at about sunset – too late to be asked to do any work in return for his tea, sugar and flour.

The places where country folk live and work are often not officially named districts, so in typically practical Australian fashion some areas are identified by the vegetation they contain, as in the following:

the brigalow　this is a kind of acacia or wattle – not an unpleasant tree but one that's difficult to clear for farming because of its habit of suckering. Cattle tend to get lost in it too, and only eat the foliage when they're almost starving. It can also cause **brigalow itch**, a form of dermatitis.

the mallee　the mallee can refer to a number of semi-arid areas in New South Wales, South Australia and Western Australia, but is particularly applied to a region in Victoria where mallee gums grow. The mallee is a species of eucalypt that appears to have no trunk at all (the branches rise straight from the ground), but which does have an enormous and tough root system, a fact that has broken the hearts of many farmers who have tried to dig it out. Mallee root makes good firewood, though, as it's hard and slow-burning.

CLICK GO THE SHEARS

Shearers, the men and women who shear sheep, have their own jargon – masses of it. The champion shearer in each shearing shed, for instance, is called the **gun shearer** or **ringer**. Some other examples are provided by an old song which celebrates this sweaty job, 'Click Go the Shears Boys':

> The ringer looks around and is beaten by a blow,
> And curses the old swaggie with the bare-bellied yeo.

The **ringer** in this instance is beaten by one blow – that is, one stroke of the shears. And what's worse, he is beaten by an old **swaggie**, a nobody in the shearer's world. The **swaggie** won by shearing a **bare-bellied yeo** – a ewe that has defective wool growth that makes the wool come off easily.

> ❝ WOOP-WOOP
> — A FAR AWAY PLACE IN THE
> MIDDLE OF NOWHERE ❞

the saltbush   saltbush only grows in salty, semidesert regions of central Australia where pretty much nothing else will. Despite the obvious drawbacks of its taste, sheep will eat it.

the scrub   land covered by shrubby bushes, often dense to the point of being impenetrable and indicating poor soil. To be 'out in the scrub' or 'the scrubs' is to be somewhere unpleasantly remote.

the spinifex   this spiny, tussocky grass is mostly found in arid zones of Australia

The city

The city is sometimes referred to by country people as the **big smoke** and its inhabitants as **city slickers**. Australians who are fleeing the cities to live in small, slow-paced towns by the sea are taking part in a modern phenomenon known as a **sea change** (or if it's a small slow-paced inland town, **tree change**).

the CBD   the Central Business District – traditionally anywhere within walking distance of the main post office (called the General Post Office or **GPO**)

the city   this is an important and confusing term in Australian English and has various meanings: it can refer, for example, to either the whole of Melbourne or just the Central Business District. A city can also be a large region – you can be driving through the middle of nowhere and find a sign which states that you're now in the City of Bullamakanka. There's a basic distinction between a city,

GOING TO TOWN

Sometimes you'll hear people say they're 'going to town' for the day, by which they mean they're going to the city centre. They could live 10 minutes away but they will still say this.

which is very big, and a town, which can be big or small but which is considered less important than a city.

the inner city/suburbs this is the ring of suburbs reaching from just beyond the CBD out to about 7km from the GPO. In Sydney, however, the concept of the inner suburb is more complicated – most people, for example, don't consider North Sydney (just across the Harbour Bridge from the CBD) to be an inner suburb.

the suburbs beyond the inner suburbs are the suburbs proper. The **burbs** have long been the stuff of many middle-class dreams, but are often dismissed by inner-city dwellers as conservative and tediously homogeneous. People who live in the outer suburbs are (stereotypically) considered uncool, **bevans**, **bogans**, **westies**, etc – the antithesis of the inner-city crowd.

The good, the bad & the bludger

Whether they live in the bush, on the beach, in the inner city or in the burbs, Australians generally like to think of themselves as honest, hard-working souls. Perhaps for this reason, Australian English provides terms to make unambiguous distinctions between good and bad people and their actions.

'Good' people can be described in the following ways:

fair dinkum honest, genuine. This expression, which also means 'the truth', comes from the Lancashire dialect in the UK and refers to the basic notion that a fair day's work (or **dinkum**) demands a fair day's pay. Other terms with a similar meaning include **the drum, the full two bob, the good guts, the good oil, the griff, the real thing, the straight wire** and **true dinks**.

good sport   even someone who has never played sport can be described as a good sport – it means they are good-natured and uncomplaining, accept teasing cheerfully, and are willing to give something or someone a go

plays it straight   is fair. Alternatively, **plays fair** or **plays with a straight bat**.

tall poppy   a high-achiever. The **tall poppy** is invariably at risk of being cut down by a **knocker** (critic).

upfront   honest and/or blunt. Alternatively, **above board**, dinky-di, **lays it on the line**, **ridgy-didge** or **straight up and down**.

> ❝ BULLSHIt ARtISt
> — A SCAMMER; OR A LIAR OR
> EXAGGERATOR ❞

'Bad' people, or **mongrels** in old-fashioned parlance, take just as many forms. One of the most prominent types is the **bullshit artist** who lies in order to lure you into his latest **lurk** or **rort**. (People are sometimes also labelled bullshit artists when it's thought they're exaggerating or bending the truth.) To **rort the system** is to twist the rules or procedures of an organisation in a manner which is either illegal or bordering on it, for one's own advantage. This used to be popularly thought a political speciality but has spread. **Rorts** are also known as **scams** or **shonks**. Dubious schemes and plans often sound a bit **suss** (suspect), but sometimes you have to **suss them out**

OH THE BOGANITY

Once a term for a specific group of working-class, ugg-boot and stretch-denim wearing, heavy-metal listening, Winfield-Blue smoking yobbos, the word 'bogan' has become an elastic term meaning something like 'anyone who's less cultured and sophisticated than I (the speaker) am'. After a couple of decades of rising use, it's finally made it to Oxford Dictionary respectability and has a number of ancillary uses, the most useful of which is 'cashed-up bogan' (CUB) – a newly rich bogan with a penchant for conspicuous consumption (often applied to sporting celebrities).

(investigate them) in order to realise this. Other descriptions of 'bad' people include the following:

bludger   person who lives off other people, either financially or emotionally. A bludger can be said to **put the bite on**, **put the fangs into** or **put the nips into** someone. A particularly heinous type is the **dole bludger**, who lives on government benefits because it's easier than working.

cadger   a less common word for a **bludger**, a bloodsucker or parasite

dobber   person who reports things like **scams**, **rorts** and **bludging**. One of the contradictions of Australian culture is that those who turn 'bad' people in are often disliked, because they're seen to have somehow offended against the spirit of mateship.

yobbos/yobs   uncouth, aggressive people with no subtlety to their antisocial behaviour

Home & family

Middle-class family life in Australia used to be manacled to the notion of the quarter-acre block, where mum, dad and their 1.7 kids would set up home and live the Australian Dream. 'Family' is still a buzzword in contemporary Australian life and the quarter-acre block still lures many parents and their broods out to the suburbs, with their reassuring similitude of housing. But increasingly, homes and their immediate environments take many forms. Following is a list of common housing and residential area terms.

> **❝ DUNNY, CRAPPER, THUNDERBOX**
> **— TOILET ❞**

apartment usually refers to an upmarket (often inner-city) flat, although the term is starting to spread to include all kinds of flats. A **studio apartment** is a small one-room flat.

brick-veneer house a home with a timber frame and brick exterior. This style of house dominates the burbscape.

California bungalow the California bungalow is another of the basic house styles of the Australian suburb, and was imported from the goldfields of California in the 1850s. It's typically one storey high with a low-pitched roof, a buttress-like stone or pebble chimney, and a front gable overhanging a verandah upheld by massive stone pillars.

dunny toilet. Also called a **crapper, lav, loo** and **thunderbox**. Plumbers are occasionally called **dunny divers**.

duplex this can be a two-storey block of flats or home units, each dwelling occupying one floor, or a house divided in two vertically

façadism this practice involves retaining the façade of an old building while constructing a new one behind it

Federation-style characterised by a red-brick exterior, front verandahs with decorative timber railings, terracotta roof tiles and chimney pots. Houses built in this style date back to between 1890 and 1920.

flat this is the basic term for a living space in an apartment building or divided house

footpath pedestrian path on the side of a road (called a 'sidewalk' in North America and a 'pavement' in the UK)

granny flat a small building in the backyard of a house which can be used as a separate dwelling. Quaintly called a **chalet** in Tasmania.

laneway narrow street at the rear of a block of houses, usually originally designed to allow access to garbage collection and, in the days before sewerage, nightsoil collectors (when they were often called 'dunny lanes')

nature strip a (usually grassy) strip by the side of the road, often between the road and the **footpath**. Called a 'verge' in most other English-speaking countries.

Queenslander common in Queensland (and Darwin, before Cyclone Tracy blew them all down in 1974), these timber homes have wide verandahs and are built on stilts to make the most of cool breezes

semi-detached house one of a pair of houses joined by a common wall

share house a house shared by a group of (usually young) people. It's particularly common in the inner city.

terrace house a house joined by common walls to the houses on either side. Terraces were basically workers' housing of the 19th and early 20th century but have become popular among inner-city dwellers. Paddington terrace houses in Sydney, and those in Melbourne's Carlton, are particularly famous for the charm of the iron lace on their balconies and the wealth of their owners.

unit   a small house sharing a block of land with a number of others

villa   a classier kind of modern terrace house, slightly bigger and with better bathrooms and kitchens

weatherboard   a house clad with overlapping timber boards

Hollies

Anyone taking a **hollie** (holiday) in Australia will find that the country's geographical diversity is reflected in the diversity of places to stay. Besides the usual hotels and motels, travellers can stay in a **pub** (public house) or a **B&B** (bed and breakfast, where breakfast is included in the room rate). Those looking for a place to bunk down in the outback will come across the **donga**, a small room containing only a bed which is sometimes

MOVING HOUSE

An established business in Queensland is the transplanting of **Queenslander** houses from the original block to another, be it in a neighbouring suburb or a faraway town. As if in a supermarket, buyers meander through rows of these charming timber houses propped up on bricks and choose their dream home. For a fee, the house is sliced in two, lifted onto wide trucks, driven – slowly – to the empty block and 'rebuilt'. Voila!

stand-alone but more often lies within a row of similar rooms that collectively resemble a large metal shipping container; donga is also the name given to the transportable building containing such rooms. Some holiday-makers choose to take their accommodation with them, hooking up a **caravan** (what Americans call a '(house) trailer') to their car.

> ❝ PANEL VAN
> — CLASSIC AUSSIE VEHICLE ❞

On the frog & toad

Keen drivers can circumnavigate Australia on the road known as Highway 1, and for an encore can cross the continent from north to south on the Stuart Highway, which links Darwin in the Northern Territory with Port Augusta in South Australia. Once you've got those two trips on nice paved roads out of the way, it's time to strap yourself in and go four-wheel-driving. Australia is criss-crossed with rugged, rutted dirt tracks, which usually began their lives as cattle droving trails. Among the most famous are the 1700km Canning Stock Route and the Birdsville Track.

A common sight on Australian roads is the **ute** (utility truck), which has a rectangular rear tray for transporting goods and equipment; it's also the natural home of cattle dogs like the blue heeler. This is also the only place in the world other than New Zealand where you'll see the **panel van**, a two-door van that looks like a swollen station wagon. On the highway, prepare to be intimidated by passing **road trains**. These are semitrailer trucks (prime movers) towing up to four trailers – once they've picked up speed on the open road, they're notoriously reluctant to slow down for anything!

Here are some more driving terms:

click	kilometres, as in 'How many clicks to the next town?'
interstate	in or to another Australian state, as in 'Laura's gone interstate'
median strip	the (usually raised) dividing area between opposing traffic lanes
offsider	companion
park	in relation to driving, this means 'parking space', as in 'I'll try and find a park'
petrol	called 'gas(oline)' in North America

From kindy to uni

Australian education generally begins with **kindergarten** or **kindy**, also known as **preschool**. This can comprise the first year of primary school, or the first year may be called **prep** (preparatory). Primary school then generally takes schoolchildren from year one (or first grade) to year six (sixth grade). After this comes **secondary school**, more commonly known as **high school**, which usually lasts from year 7 to year 12. In some rural areas there is a state-run institution called an **area school** or **district school** which provides both primary and secondary education. Also, in some states and territories high school finishes at year 10 and is followed by a **matriculation college** or **secondary college** which looks after years 11 and 12.

The celebrations marking secondary school graduations are known as **schoolies**. The traditional hub of these festivities is the Gold Coast in Queensland, where teenagers flock in their thousands to create alcohol-fuelled chaos during **Schoolies' Week** in November. (An unsavoury side-effect of which is **toolies**, predatory males past high school age who attend in order to attempt picking up drunken teenage girls.) Students who are accepted into tertiary education will move on to **uni** (university).

The rigours of the primary school day in Australia are alleviated somewhat by a mid-morning break known either as **little lunch**, **playlunch** or **recess**. This is when children stampede into the **canteen** or **tuckshop**, a shop at the school which sells food. Tuckshops were once weighted towards snack foods like pies and chips but in response to burgeoning obesity rates over the last decade or so have generally become much more health-conscious. But as much as kids look forward to recess or lunchtime, nothing compares to getting an **early mark** – to be allowed to go home from school early.

> **❝ RATBAG, SCUM, DRONGO, SILLY OLD BUGGER**
> **— PARLIAMENTARY INSULTS ❞**

One of the more popular schoolyard games is **British bulldog**, usually played by a large group of boys. One boy stands in the middle of the playground and while the others run past him from one end of the playground to the other he tries to tackle (throw his arms around or bring down) one of them. The captured boy then joins his captor in trying to tackle other boys and the process is repeated until everyone has been tackled. The last boy caught stands in the middle when the next game starts. A less rough version of this game is called **red rover**, which involves tagging (touching) rather than tackling.

A less pleasurable playground activity is the **emu parade**, where teachers supervise a group of kids in picking up litter around the school. When this is undertaken as a punishment, it's called **scab duty**. Someone who rarely (if ever) is forced to do scab duty is the **conchie**. Short for 'conscientious', this is a disparaging term for those students who always try to do their utmost best at school, often becoming **teacher's pets**. They would never, for instance, think of **wagging** (intentionally missing school).

Work & politics

The Australian workplace has had its fair share of both success and scandal. The 1970s, for instance, did nothing to improve the image of Australia's corporate accountants. It was during this decade that a number of hard-working accountants (aka **number crunchers** or **bean counters**) devised some intricate, though not technically illegal, methods for minimising company tax. These were called **bottom-of-the-harbour** schemes because the records relating to these dubious transactions were often destroyed or, as it were, 'sent to the bottom of Sydney Harbour'. The expression is now used to describe any **shonky** (dubious) business arrangements.

Australia's political realm is also marvellously idiosyncratic. Australian politicians seem to positively pride themselves on inventing colourful terms of abuse for each other. When the ABC (the Australian Broadcasting Corporation) began broadcasting in Asia, it found that **Parliamentary Question Time** was

'IF THE DUMMIES OPPOSITE WILL JUST SHUT UP'

Former Prime Minister Paul Keating was the acknowledged master of the political insult. Here are some of his finer slurs:
'The Opposition crowd could not raffle a chook in a pub'
'The little desiccated coconut is under pressure...'
'What we have got is a dead carcass, swinging in the breeze...'
'I am not like the Leader of the Opposition. I did not slither out of the Cabinet room like a mangy maggot...'
'...he is all tip and no iceberg'
'...(he) was like a lizard on a rock – alive, but looking dead'

HOUSEHOLD NAMES: POLITICIANS

Bob Hawke

Labor Prime Minister 1983–91. A former union leader famous for his colourful personal life and his assertion immediately after Australia won the 1983 America's Cup (a yacht race) that 'Anyone who sacks a bloke because he doesn't turn up for work today is a bum!'

John Howard

Liberal Prime Minister 1996–2007. He presided over the modern era of conservative politics, with strong links to the neo-conservatives in the US administration and a reverence for his predecessor Robert Menzies.

Paul Keating

Labor Prime Minister 1991–96. Among other things, famous for putting his hand on the Queen's back and being labelled the 'Lizard of Oz' by British tabloids.

Robert Menzies

Prime Minister 1939–41 and 1949–66. He helped form the Liberal Party and was their leader for his second period as PM, for which he still holds the record as Australia's longest serving PM. An avowed monarchist, and the Liberals' greatest icon.

Gough Whitlam

Labor Prime Minister 1972–75. A controversial figure adored by the left and deplored by conservatives, his Government was dismissed by the Governor General in 1975 in an act that still raises political hackles on both sides.

one of the most popular shows; viewers from Singapore to the Philippines apparently got a kick out of the entertaining abuse. **Drongo**, **dingbat**, **great galah**, **idiot**, **ratbag**, **scum**, **sheep** and **silly old bugger** are some of the terms let fly from the parliamentary benches.

....

Love & pashes

Australians are relatively uninhibited about love and dating. This is not to say they aren't conservative (many are) but younger people in particular are likely to be upfront about their feelings, or at least their desires. Still, not all locals are comfortable with intimacy – stereotypically, the laconic, blokey nature of many Australian men means they tend to restrain, if not bury, their emotions.

You might come across one of the following terms in discussions on love and sex:

bonk	have sex with (**bonk buddies** are casual sex partners)
crack onto	chat up (someone)
frenchie	condom
in the raw/nud	naked
pash (on)	kiss passionately
quickie	anything done in a hurry; quick sex
randy	lustful – thus not a popular choice for a child's name in Australia
root	have sex with (a fairly coarse term)
shag	have sex with
spunk	good-looking person of either sex; similarly spunk-rat, most commonly refers to men
starkers	naked

The real national anthem

The Australian national anthem is 'Advance Australia Fair', which replaced the former anthem, 'God Save the Queen', in 1984. Adult Australians rarely find themselves needing to sing the anthem, however, and as a result often struggle to remember the words – after an enthusiastic start, it often becomes a musical mumble.

A song that Australians tend to know better – and usually sing with more gusto – is the unofficial national anthem, 'Waltzing Matilda'. The words contain a whole swathe of Australian colloquialisms from the 19th century:

> **Once a jolly swagman camped by a billabong**
> **Under the shade of a coolibah tree**

The **swagman** is a tramp or wanderer who carries a **swag** – his clothes, cooking implements and so on tied up in a blanket or bedroll. The **billabong** is a waterhole in a river that is otherwise usually dry. The **coolibah** tree is a species of eucalypt found in inland Australia, often in areas which get flooded from time to time (hence the location near the billabong).

> **And he sang as he watched and waited till his billy boiled**
> **You'll come a-waltzing matilda with me**

The **billy** is a tin container used for boiling water for tea. No one is sure where the word comes from but it could come from the Scottish word 'bally', meaning bucket. The origin of the expression **waltzing matilda**, meaning being 'on the road' (as a tramp), is also uncertain. It probably dates back to a German influence on the goldfields, as 'Matilda' is the German equivalent of a **swag**: the 'girl' a man sleeps with when he's alone on the road. Also, the expression 'to waltz' was used to describe German apprentices moving from one town to another to learn their trade.

> Down came a jumbuck to drink at that billabong
> Up jumped the swagman and grabbed him with glee
> And he sang as he shoved that jumbuck in his tuckerbag
> You'll come a-waltzing matilda with me

The **jumbuck** is a sheep. This is thought to be Aboriginal pidgin for 'jump up', which is presumably what was most immediately noticeable about sheep. The **tuckerbag** is a bag for holding food. (**Tucker** is a British schoolboy word for food which still survives in Australian English.)

> Up rode the squatter mounted on his thoroughbred
> Down came the troopers – one, two, three
> Whose that jolly jumbuck you've got in your tuckerbag
> You'll come a-waltzing matilda with me

In this verse, the strong arm of the law, in the form of **troopers** (mounted police officers), arrives to arrest the swagman for stealing the jumbuck. **Squatters** were originally pioneer settlers on land the government had not got around to officially allocating yet. They became wealthy landowners, part of the **squattocracy**, the new aristocracy of pastoral Australia. This squatter rides a thoroughbred horse and seems to be the lawful owner of the jumbuck.

> Up jumped the swagman and sprang into the billabong
> You'll never catch me alive said he
> And his ghost may be heard as you pass by that billabong
> You'll come a-waltzing matilda with me

❝ BILLABONG
— WATERHOLE ❞

Dangerous Australians

Australia is home to some of the most poisonous creatures in the world. ('How on earth', foreigners have been known to ask 'have you survived here all these years?') There are three main categories. Firstly, the spiders, which include the following:

funnel-webs a big black hairy spider around 6cm across, common in the Sydney area. Bites can be fatal.

redbacks a 2cm to 3cm-long black spider with a bright red stripe on the back. Bites are painful but rarely fatal.

whitetails a small grey or reddish-brown spider with a long cylindrical body that has a whitish spot on the tip. Again, their bites are painful, but are not dangerous.

Secondly, of course, there are the snakes. All of the following are highly venomous:

black snakes (genus *Pseudechis*) including the mulga or 'king brown' snake and the red-bellied black snake

brown snakes (genus *Pseudonaja*) found throughout mainland Australia

taipans (*Oxyuranus* species) a more aggressive snake from the north and northeast coast

tiger snakes (*Notechis* species) usually but not always striped, found along the southeast coast of Australia

Although snakes and spiders should certainly be treated with respect, there have been no deaths as a result of spider bites for several decades, and there are only a handful of snakebite fatalities each year.

The third category of poisonous critters is the **stingers**, including such nasties as the **blue-ringed octopus** and the **bluebottle**. The most deadly stinger is the **box jellyfish** of northern Australia. Its stings are excruciating and require immediate treatment with antivenom.

EATING, DRINKING & MAKING MERRY

Look out for these...

CLASSIC PHRASE:
HAPPY LITTLE VEGEMITES
Well-behaved children like those in a famous 1950s ad for the salty breakfast spread

TRY THIS ONE:
MY SHOUT!
When you say this in the pub, everybody's your friend

USE WITH CAUTION:
MIDDY, SCHOONER, POT
There are different names for the same sized glass of beer, depending on which state you're in

MISUNDERSTANDINGS:
CHIPS
In Australia these might be either potato crisps or hot chips (French fries)

EATING, DRINKING & MAKING MERRY

Twenty years ago, many Australians would have sat down each night to the traditional, Anglo-derived dinner of 'meat and three veg' followed by stewed fruit (out of a tin) and custard or jelly (out of a packet). Happily, since that time the culinary offerings of Australia's multicultural society have been enthusiastically accepted, and these days a standard home-cooked dinner is more likely to involve some kind of pasta or stir-fry. In fact, in recent years Australia has become a foodie's paradise as people have become more adventurous, palates more sophisticated and what was previously the provenance only of gourmets has become mainstream.

Australians eat foodstuffs from around the world, but you'll increasingly also find Australian native or 'bush' foods like wattleseeds, macadamia nuts, kangaroo, crocodile, emu and bush tomatoes. Witchetty (**witjuti**) grubs remain a delicacy only indigenous peoples are brave enough to enjoy.

> **" DOG'S EYE WITH DEAD HORSE**
> **— PIE WITH SAUCE "**

There is plenty of interesting eating to enjoy, not just in the major cities but in many regional towns too. The same goes for Australian liquids, with international-quality coffee blends, boutique breweries and award-winning vineyards all doing their bit to invigorate the palate.

Eating

Mealtimes in Australia almost need a mini-menu themselves:

brekkie   breakfast. On workdays, this commonly consists of things like cereal or muesli with milk (and possibly fruit or yoghurt) or toast, butter and **Vegemite** (see p72), accompanied by a simple **cuppa** (tea or coffee).

morning tea   generally **bickies** and a **cuppa** with the occasional indulgence in a cake or bun

brunch   a leisurely combination of breakfast and lunch, usually a weekend ritual that involves more elaborate cooked breakfast dishes (eggs with various side dishes, pancakes, and so on)

lunch   often consists of one of the endless variations on the theme of some kind of bread product with fillings – whether it be a plain old **sanga** or **sarnie** (sandwich), a **roll** (bread roll) or a filled **pide** (Turkish bread, pronounced 'peedeh'), **focaccia** (Italian bread), bagel or **wrap** (flat-bread of some kind wrapped around a filling). Australians also love to 'do' lunch at a cafe or restaurant.

afternoon tea   at work, for most Australians this is a repeat of morning tea. For a luxury treat, though, try the five-star hotels in major cities for a Victorian-era-style **spread** of tea, cakes and petite sandwiches.

dinner/tea   the main meal of the day. 'Tea', the Northern English term, is becoming less common. Sometimes referred to as **din-dins**, mainly by kids.

❝ CHEW'N'SPEW

— FAST FOOD **❞**

Other Aussie terms relating to meals and eating out include:

BYO; Bring Your Own   (alcoholic) drinks to a restaurant or party

chew'n'spew   general name for fast food

corkage   the fee charged by restaurants for BYO wines

counter meal/tea   a pub meal, though not necessarily eaten at the **counter** (or bar) and usually cheap – though lots of city pubs have gone upmarket. Standard pub meals include chicken parmigiana (a **parma**), fish and chips, steaks, **bangers and mash** (sausages and mashed potatoes), roast dinners and various pasta dishes. Also called a **counterie**.

Devonshire tea   scones ('biscuits' to North Americans) with jam and cream and a pot of hot tea, as known to the British as a 'cream tea', originating from the county of Devon

entrée   on a restaurant menu this is a starter, not a main course as in some other countries

esky   portable ice-box

junk food   general term for any kind of food which is high in accessibility but low in nutrients, like pizza, **Macca's** (food from McDonald's), **lollies** and fried food (or **hot'n'greasies**) such as chips or **dimmies** (dim sims, a kind of large meat dumpling). Fried fish and chips are also sometimes called **fish'n'greasies** or **chish and fips**.

munchies   snacks like chips, pies, chocolate bars and so on fall into the category of munchies. To have an **attack of the munchies** is to suffer sudden severe pangs of hunger, a fate known to befall pot smokers in particular.

nibblies   finger food like nuts, chips and hors d'oeuvres, nibbled on at parties or special **do's** (functions)

nosh   an old-fashioned word for food, as in 'Do you feel like some nosh?' In times past people have also used the words **chow**, **grub** and **tucker** to mean the same thing.

(a) spread   a magnificent offering of food and drink, the proverbial groaning board. A spread offers you the chance of a **blow-out**, **beanfeast** or **pig-out**.

Aussie tucker

The Aussie meat pie (in rhyming slang, a **dog's eye**) is a hand-held affair found in pie-warmers in **milk bars**, bakeries, highway **servos** (service stations, aka petrol stations) and even some upmarket cafes, and sold by the thousands at sporting events. A day at the **footy** just wouldn't be the same without a pie'n'sauce (ie ketchup). They're notoriously hotter inside than you'd expect and come with the risk of second-degree burns to the roof of the mouth. The traditional beef pie has been supplemented over the years with 'gourmet' concoctions featuring ingredients like Thai curry chicken or beef burgundy and even vegetarian creations like corn, cheese and asparagus.

Also, when in South Australia, keep your eyes peeled and taste buds primed for the state's native **pie floater** – a meat pie sitting in a bowl of thick pea soup. Don't be alarmed; many people consider these very tasty, especially on a freezing night or after a few hours of drinking. They're sold on Adelaide city streets from pie-carts.

Here's a list of other typical Australian edibles:

barra	barramundi (fish)
battered sav	saveloy in batter, sometimes called a **dagwood dog** or a **dippy dog** (SA)
bickie	sweet biscuit
brown bread	wholemeal bread
bum-nuts	eggs; also called **cackleberries**, **googies** or **googs** (the 'oo' as in 'put') and **henfruits**
caulie	cauliflower
cheese'n'greens	cheese platter
Chiko roll	a deep-fried bigger cousin of the Chinese spring roll

chips	either potato crisps or French fries, though the latter may be thicker than a classic French fry
chook	chicken
coconut ice	sweet confection consisting of pink and white blocks of dried coconut and sugar
a cut lunch	sandwiches
dead horse	tomato sauce (ie ketchup)
dodger	bread

> ❝ BUM-NUtS, CACKLEBERRIES, GOOGIES
> — EGGS ❞

drumstick	chicken leg
flake	fillet of shark, a popular choice in fish and chip shops
golden syrup	sugar cane syrup
hedgehog	a chocolate slice incorporating crushed biscuits
jam	sweet fruit preserve – North Americans call it 'jelly'
jelly	gelatine dessert – 'jello' in North America
marge	margarine
mince	called 'hamburger meat' in North America
minimum chips	the standard serving of chips available in a fish and chip shop
moo juice	milk; also called **cow juice**

muddie	mud crab (Queensland)
muesli	granola
mushies	mushrooms
nana	banana (pronounced 'narna')
pav	pavlova – a traditional Australian meringue dessert
pikelets	little pancakes
prawn	any of a number of species of edible marine crustacean, whether big or tiny
rat coffin	minced meat pie

> **❝ BANGERS, MYSTERY BAGS, SNAGS**
> **— SAUSAGES ❞**

sausage roll	meat wrapped in flaky pastry; you'll find them beside meat pies in pie-warmers
scones	plain, doughy cakes, called 'biscuits' in the USA
silverbeet	also known as (Swiss) chard
snorkers	sausages; also called **bangers**, **mystery bags**, **snags** and **snarlers**
spag bol	spaghetti bolognese; you may hear this dish referred to as **spaghetti blow-your-nose**
spud	potato
strawbs	strawberries
surf'n'turf	a slab of steak topped with seafood, a typical pub dish

APPETISING EXPRESSIONS

Here are a few Aussie expressions you might hear relating to hunger and thirst.

Hunger

I wouldn't mind a bite.
How about a quick bite?
I could eat a horse and chase the jockey.
My stomach thinks my throat's cut.
I could eat the crutch out of a low-flying duck.
I've got the munchies.

Thirst (usually for beer)

I've got a thirst you could photograph.
Your tongue's hanging out.
What about a drop, mate?
How about wetting your whistle?

The second drink

That one didn't touch the sides.
Tide's gone out.
How about anotherie?
I could go another one.

sweets	dessert
toastie	toasted sandwich
yum cha	Chinese restaurant meal in which trolleys loaded with small dishes (such as dumplings) cruise the tables, diners choosing from them as they pass

Classic Aussie foods

There are some food items which have become such a part of the Australian way of life that most locals couldn't imagine doing without them:

Aeroplane jelly   comes in pretty packets and in a range of flavours such as 'tropical', mango and lilly pilly (a native fruit). Its famous advertising jingle ('I like Aeroplane jelly, Aeroplane jelly for me!') has been around since the 1930s.

Arnott's milk arrowroot biscuit   a plain sweet biscuit which is the starting point for a number of desserts or confections

Cherry Ripe   Australia's oldest brand of chocolate bar, consisting of cherries and coconut coated in dark chocolate

Coon cheese   a kind of basic processed cheddar or 'tasty' cheese. It's named after its creator, but can cause consternation among US visitors.

Iced Vo-Vo   a sweet biscuit topped with fondant, jam and coconut

Sao biscuit   a large flaky cracker, traditionally eaten either smothered in butter and **Vegemite** or topped with cheese; the **Salada** is given similar treatment

Tim Tam   one of Australia's favourite biscuits, the Tim Tam has a layer of chocolate cream between two chocolate biscuits, with a chocolate coating. The infamous 'Tim Tam Slam' involves biting off diagonally opposite corners of the biscuit, sucking hot tea or coffee through them like a straw, and then cramming the whole biscuit into your mouth before it disintegrates. Don't attempt this in polite society!

Vegemite   a salty, vitamin-rich yeast extract from the same family as Promite and Marmite, and a byproduct of beer brewing (so there's quite a bit of it around); commonly spread on toast or crackers. Its famous TV ad from the 1950s has given rise to the expression 'happy little Vegemites' – contented and well-behaved children like the ones that appeared in the ad.

Violet Crumble   a chocolate bar consisting of honeycomb covered in chocolate

Australian childhoods are sweetened by various sugary treats:

chocolate crackles	balls of puffed rice mixed with chocolate and coconut
cordial	sweet, concentrated syrup you mix with water to create a drink
fairy bread	buttered bread sprinkled with **hundreds and thousands**
fairy floss	known as 'candy floss' in other countries
hundreds and thousands	tiny balls of multicoloured sugar used in cake decoration and to make **fairy bread**
icy pole	frozen sweet flavoured water on a stick
little boys	small frankfurts; also called **cheerios**
lollies	confectionery or sweets
lolly water	soft drink (see below)
soft drink	carbonated nonalcoholic drink

> **HAPPY LITTLE VEGEMITES**
> — WELL-BEHAVED CHILDREN LIKE
> THOSE IN A FAMOUS 1950S AD FOR
> SALTY BREAKFAST SPREAD

Foreign influences

Not so long ago, **billy tea**, **damper**, **pavlova**, **pie floaters** and **Vegemite** were seen as the only Australian contributions to world cuisine. These days, seekers of a **fair dinkum** Aussie dining experience might find themselves joining the Sunday **arvo** throng in Chinatown for yum cha, delighting in an Italian, Greek, Turkish or Thai banquet, or dining out on Vietnamese food or snap-fresh sashimi and sushi. Australian migrants have endowed the national cuisine with all the above and more – great coffee, every kind of cheese, superb fresh and cured meats, olives and olive oil, fresh Asian vegies like bok choy and gai larn, and feisty spices.

Coffee

If it weren't for the great postwar wave of Italian migration, Australians might still be making coffee out of bottled essence or instant powder. Nowadays, no city restaurant or cafe would survive without its espresso machine and well-trained staff to crank out cups of java. So worshipped has coffee become in the modern Australian lifestyle that rising real estate prices can be tracked merely by counting the number of espresso machines per head in any given city suburb. And God help you if you're out to impress anyone with social pretensions and you don't know your latte from your macchiato. The exception tends to be remote areas, where the choice in (instant) coffee will probably be limited to 'Black or white, love?'

Here are some of the more usual brews available:

caffe latte   (often just called a 'latte') half espresso, half steamed milk: slightly frothy and usually served in a glass

cappuccino   (aka 'capp') one-third espresso with one-third steamed milk and one-third milk froth, usually topped with sprinkled chocolate powder. Don't be alarmed if your **capp** arrives without the **chockie** though – it just means you're in a cafe that chooses to serve cappuccinos as the Italians do.

double espresso   the post-business lunch power jolt: two short blacks in one cup

flat white   two-thirds espresso, one-third steamed milk: no froth, hence the word 'flat'. A flat white is usually served in a cup, if only to distinguish it from a **latte**.

SOUVLAKI CITY

Melbourne has the largest Greek population in Australia (and one of the largest in the world), so you won't have any trouble finding souvlaki, taramasalata, ouzo and Greek newspapers – especially in Lonsdale St in the CBD, Melbourne's 'Little Athens'.

long black   order this if you've got the caff-crave for a basic black espresso coffee topped with hot water

long macchiato   (long mac) a long black with, as the word 'macchiato' translates, just a 'stain' of cold milk

short black   small strong espresso

short macchiato   (short mac) an espresso with a 'stain' of cold milk

Then there are the variations. Cappuccinos or lattes also come in soy and **skinny** versions, made with soy and low-fat milk respectively. Any coffee can be ordered **decaf**, too – made with decaffeinated coffee beans. And finally, there's the **babyccino** (milk froth in a tiny cup, topped with sprinkled chocolate powder) – cafe-society training-wheels for kids.

Getting on the piss

Beer, the amber nectar

Lager is the dominant style in Australia and is served ice-cold – a bottle of beer is sometimes just called a **coldie**, as in 'Jeez, I could murder a coldie right now'. States remain somewhat loyal to their local beers, but the growing dominance of multinational brewers and distributors means that usually you'll also find interstate and international beers on tap. Even so, in a country pub you may find the choice is Brand X or Brand Y, both owned by Foster's or Lion Nathan. Whether it's VB (Victoria Bitter) in Victoria, Swan in Western Australia, XXXX (pronounced 'four ex') in Queensland or West End in South Australia, the irony of the state brews is that they often don't taste all that different when poured into a glass at a chilly temperature.

> **BLOTTO, LEGLESS, RAT-ARSED, PISSED AS A PARROT**
> — DRUNK

You'll find more varied flavours among the produce of Tasmania's Cascade Brewery (Australia's oldest), South Australia's Coopers Brewery and New South Wales' James Squire. In recent years there has been an explosion of microbreweries, led by Little Creatures (in Western Australia) and Mountain Goat (in Victoria). Most microbrewers concentrate on ales, stouts and pilseners, and there's a huge range of interesting and outlandish beers to be sampled in the country's more adventurous pubs and bottle shops.

While most Australians agree on the worthiness of drinking beer, the different states have different words for talking about it. See the Beer Menu, opposite, for a short guide to some of the state-specific terms relating to beer drinking.

At the boozer

A pub is the best place in which to start sampling the various styles and sizes of Aussie beer. A pub can be anything from a small bush shanty with a bar and verandah to a glossy, groovy,

BEER MENU

In a pub

bobby	6oz glass in Western Australia
butcher	6oz glass in South Australia
glass	5oz glass in Western Australia
grog	general term for beer or spirits
handle	medium-sized beer glass with a handle
middy	10oz glass in New South Wales and Queensland; 7oz glass in Western Australia
pot	10oz glass in Western Australia, Victoria and Queensland
schooner	15oz glass in New South Wales and Queensland; 10oz glass in South Australia
ten	10oz glass of beer in the Northern Territory (you can also order a **fifteen**)

Takeaway

Darwin stubby	reputedly the largest beer bottle in the world at 2.25 litres
dead marine	an empty beer bottle
echo	small beer bottle in South Australia
sixpack	a pack of six bottles
slab	a pack of 24 cans or bottles
stubby	small beer bottle
tallie	large beer bottle (pronounced 'tawlie'); also **longneck**
tinnie	a tin of beer; also called a **tube**

cosmopolitanised city number. If it's close to home and a favoured haunt then it's known as **the local**; other pet names include **the rubbidy** (rhyming slang – **rubbidy dub** means 'pub'), **the pisser** or **the boozer**. Most pubs have a **bottle shop** (or **bottle-o**) to sell takeaway beer, wine and so on, and it often has a drive-through facility. There are also **bottle shops** which operate independently of pubs.

> **❝ tHE RUBBIDY, tHE PISSER, tHE BOOZER**
>
> **— tHE PUB ❞**

Wine

Over the last few decades, Australian wine has become a multibillion-dollar industry, and new wineries and vineyards continue to spring up. Australia now ranks in the world's top five wine-exporting countries.

Before the 1970s, table wines weren't popular and sherry and port ruled supreme. Through the '80s Australia started to make a name for itself with decent cheap wines (often stored in a **bag in box** or **cask**), followed as the industry matured by serious cabernet sauvignon and shiraz varieties, which won international acclaim.

These days Australia is awash with grapes, and there are many bargains to be had, both from traditional outlets and from the increasing number of bottle shops dedicated to **cleanskins** (unbranded wines). As far as varieties go, in Australia shiraz is arguably still king. **Grange** (Penfolds Grange Hermitage) is an acknowledged world leader in the style and commands amazing prices at auction. Pinot noir is another red-hot style, so much so that a word, **pinophile**, has been coined to describe a pinot noir fanatic. However, there are still many loyal lovers of old favourites like **chardy** (chardonnay), **cab sav** (cabernet sauvignon) and **sav blanc** (sauvignon blanc), and the main party season (roughly November to January) still floats on a tide of **bubbles** (sparkling wine, aka **champers**).

Following is a list of Australia's main wine types and the regions that produce the best of each style.

Whites

chardonnay	Clare Valley (SA), Hunter Valley (NSW), Margaret River (WA), Mornington Peninsula (Vic)
pinot gris	Mornington Peninsula (Vic), Yarra Valley (Vic)
riesling	Clare Valley (SA), Eden Valley (SA)
sauvignon blanc	McLaren Vale (SA), Padthaway (SA), Yarra Valley (Vic)
semillon	Hunter Valley (NSW), McLaren Vale (SA), Margaret River (WA)
sparkling white	Adelaide Hills (SA), Tasmania, Yarra Valley (Vic)
verdelho	Hunter Valley (NSW), Margaret River (WA)

Reds

cabernet sauvignon	Coonawarra (SA), Margaret River (WA), Mudgee (NSW), Yarra Valley (Vic)
merlot	Langhorne Creek (SA), Mudgee (NSW)
pinot noir	Mornington Peninsula (Vic), Tasmania, Yarra Valley (Vic)
rosé	Barossa Valley (SA), Yarra Valley (Vic)
shiraz	Hunter Valley (NSW), McLaren Vale (SA), Mudgee (NSW), Padthaway (SA)

Following is some of the shorthand favoured by wine-lovers:

bin a term from the stock-keeping system of the Penfolds group, sometimes seen on labels (ie Bin 707)

cab merlot a blend of cabernet sauvignon and merlot

cask wine typically cheap and cheerful wine packaged in a plastic bladder inside a cardboard box (originally a whopping four litres). This Australian invention is jokingly called **chateau cardboard**, or **goon** up north.

dryland unirrigated vineyards

Grange Hermitage the nation's most famous red, created by late legendary winemaker Max Schubert

plonk cheap wine; also called **bombo**, **red ned** and **steam**

sparkling red sparkling wine made from red grapes such as shiraz, cabernet sauvignon and merlot – an Australian speciality. Also called **sparkling burgundy**.

sparkling wine slang terms for this include **bubbles**, **champers**, **fizz**, **le pop**, **shampoo** and **wa-wa juice**

vino general term for wine

Grogging on

The sheer number of terms that have been invented to describe drinkers, drinks and drinking situations gives you an idea of how intrinsic alcohol is to Australian culture:

alkie	an alcoholic
amber fluid	general term for beer; also called **slops** or **suds**
bevvie	short for 'beverage'; almost always refers to a beer
booze bus	police van used for random breath testing for alcohol
coldie	cold bottle or can of beer
drink with the flies	to drink alone

THE SHOUT

The great Australian **shout** (in rhyming slang, a **wally grout**) is a well-established custom in pubs and bars. Individuals in a group take turns buying everyone a drink – this is called buying a **round of drinks**. It can put a real strain on your wallet, depending on the size of the group and what they're drinking! It's not obligatory to take part – you can just decline the offer of a shout and buy your own drinks. Generally your nonparticipation won't bother anyone. The most important thing is not to let someone else shout you a drink if you've got no intention of reciprocating.

duck's dinner	drinking with nothing to eat
frostie	cold bottle or can of beer
grog on	to drink alcohol over quite a long period of time; also to **kick on**
heart-starter	the first alcoholic drink of the morning after a hard night's drinking
on the turps	currently in the habit of drinking vast amounts of alcohol
pig's ear	beer
pub crawl	usually a group activity, involving drinking at a number of pubs in one evening
put on the wobbly boot	to get drunk
sherbet	alcoholic beverage
sit on a beer	to drink a beer slowly
sundowner	a beer drunk in the late afternoon; mainly used in the NT
tinnie	can of beer

DRUNK AS A SKUNK

Here are some terms used to describe various levels of inebriation and other altered states:

Drunk

blotto

faceless

legless

off your face

pickled

pissed to the eyeballs

primed

shickered

sozzled

tanked

drunk as a skunk

full as a goog/boot

monged

paralytic (or para)

pissed as a fart/newt/parrot
pissed out of your brain

plastered

rat-arsed

sloshed

stewed to the gills

tight as a tick

High

bombed

high as a kite

off the planet

smashed

spacey

stoned

high

loaded

ripped

spaced out

stoked

Throw up

chunder

drive the porcelain express

do a technicolour yawn

spew

Partying on

All this booze is put to good use at a party, otherwise known as **a bit of a bash** among older Australians. The typical party-goer can be spotted mingling in someone's backyard in shorts and a T-shirt or something similarly casual, waiting for meat – and also vegie burgers or seafood these days – to finish sizzling on a **barbie**, or barbecue (which can also be the name for the event at which the barbecued meat is served). The barbecue is often attended to by males, who seem to take unusually great pride in the wielding of metal tongs.

Once upon a time in Australia, men at parties mostly just talked to other men (about sport and other blokey pursuits) and women to other women (about clothes and children, of course). This still happens occasionally but parties now are much more likely to be all-in, intermingled affairs.

> **" tECHNICOLOUR YAWN
> — voMIt "**

You might be invited to a **shindig**, **wing-ding**, **piss-up**, **booze-up** or **shivoo**, but don't fret that you're being asked to join a weird secret society – these are all words for a party. Once there, you may find yourself **making small talk**, **chewing the fat** or having a **chit-chat**, a **bit of a yarn**, a **gossip session**, a **natter** or a **yack** – in other words, a conversation. If you meet a like-minded soul you may even find yourself having a **deep and meaningful** (**d&m**) conversation about life.

Party booze & munchies

Most commonly, people either go to the party armed with **tinnies** which can be purchased in a **slab** (a carton of 24 cans of beer), or opt for the trusty cask of **plonk** (cheap wine, red or white). On arrival at the party, you'll **wet your whistle** with your first drink. Notice will have been given either verbally or in writing that the party is **BYO** (sometimes **BYOG**) – 'Bring Your Own (Grog)'. Sometimes barbecues will be labelled **BYOGM** – 'Bring Your Own Grog and Meat'. The host will then provide the extras.

For some parties (especially barbies), guests might be asked to **bring a plate** of food to share with the other guests.

It's considered rude to light up a cigarette (**ciggie**, **durry**, **fag** or **smoke**) in someone's home without asking them if it's OK.

> **❝ two-pot SCREAMER**
> **— SOMEONE WHO GEts DRUNK AFter two BEERS ❞**

Leaving the party

When you're **stuffed** or **rooted** (tired), it might be time to go. On leaving, some common expressions include: **Cheerio, I'm going to choof (off) now**, and **I'm going to chuck it in for the night**. Those who can still talk the next day can admit to a hangover with symptoms described as **blue devils**, **the DTs**, **the horrors**, **the Joe Blakes** (shakes) and **pink elephants and dingbats**. This isn't necessarily to say that the sufferer is a heavy drinker or an **alkie**, **booze artist**, **booze-hound**, **grog artist**, **hard case**, **lush**, **pisshead**, **pisspot**, **soak** or **sponge**. Some may well be **two-pot screamers** – totally **off their heads** after just two beers.

Look out for these...

CLASSIC PHRASE:
CARN!

'Come on!' as in 'Carn the Doggies!'

TRY THIS ONE:
CHEWIE ON YA BOOT!

A traditional taunt to a member of the opposing team who is trying to kick a goal

USE WITH CAUTION:
FOOTBALL

Football is Australian Rules. The other football is known as 'soccer'.

MISUNDERSTANDINGS:
THONGS

Your thongs are your flip-flops, not your collection of skimpy underwear

SPORT

Australians love watching sport. In fact, watching sport has become a sport in itself in Australia, and there are various rules to follow: ideally, find a big-screen TV at a mate's place or go to one of the pubs that get sports channels beamed in via satellite; have the fridge wellstocked with alcohol and the coffee table littered with snacks; discuss the sport at every opportunity while watching it, even if you're not that interested in proceedings, etc.

An appreciation of all things sporty is drummed into many Australians from an early age. Sportspeople give talks at schools and are held up as role models, and parents dress children up in the colours of their favourite football team and take them to games as toddlers to indoctrinate them.

❝ AVAGOYERMUG!
— HAVE A GO, YOU MUG! ❞

The main sports in Australia are **footy** (football) and cricket. The term footy, however, refers to different codes of football in different states: mainly to Australian Rules in the southern and western states and rugby league in New South Wales and Queensland. To add to the confusion, Australian soccer has rebranded itself as 'football' as well, bringing itself in line with the international name of the game.

Australian Rules football

This uniquely Australian sport, invented in 1858, is commonly referred to as **Aussie Rules** (and somewhat belittlingly and only by knockers as **aerial ping-pong**). It's played around the country in local and regional competitions as well as in the national competition, the **AFL**, or Australian Football League. The season runs from March to September, and the game is played on an oval up to 185 metres from end to end with four posts at each end: two inner, taller ones called 'goal posts', and two smaller, outer ones called 'behind posts'. Two teams of 18 (plus up to four interchange players) aim to kick an oval ball cleanly between the goal posts, thereby scoring a goal (six points). If the ball is touched on its way, or touches the post, or goes between a goal post and a behind post, it's worth a **behind** (one point). Scores of 20 goals or more by one or both teams are common. There are four quarters of 20 minutes each plus **time on** – time added due to stoppages.

> **CHEWIE ON YA BOOT!**
> — I HOPE YOU HAVE A LUMP OF CHEWING GUM STUCK ON YOUR SHOE WHICH WILL CAUSE YOU TO MISS THE GOAL!

The winning team is the one with the highest number of points at the end of the game – drawn games are rare. Tackling is fierce, and only tackling above the shoulder or below the knees and pushing in the back are banned. If the ball is kicked, goes through the air for more than 15 metres and is caught, the player who catches it is awarded what's called a **mark** by the **umpire** (referee) and takes a **free kick**. Throwing the ball is barred, but a **handball** – holding the ball in one hand and hitting it with a clenched fist – is okay.

It's traditional when attending a footy match that you **barrack** for a team as loudly as possible. In some countries **barracking** means 'abusing the opposing team', but in Australia it means to 'cheer on a team'. You'll often hear the following words being yelled out during a game:

Avagoyermug!	'Have a go, you mug!' – traditional rallying call, also used at cricket matches
Carn!	'come on', as in 'Caarn the Saints!'
Chewie on ya boot!	aimed at distracting a footballer on the verge of kicking a goal (**chewie** is chewing gum)

And football commentators and spectators use the following to describe on-field actions:

got coat-hangered	was hit by a straight arm
got dragged	was taken off the field by the coach
had a blinder	played really well
took a speccy	took a spectacular high mark

The teams

Following are the 18 teams that play in the AFL. Key venues include the MCG (Melbourne Cricket Ground, where the AFL Grand Final is held), SCG (Sydney Cricket Ground), Gabba (Brisbane Cricket Ground) and Subiaco (in Perth).

Adelaide	the Crows
Brisbane Lions	the Lions (formerly Fitzroy)
Carlton	the Blues, Blue Boys or Blue Baggers
Collingwood	the Magpies, Maggies or Pies
Essendon	the Bombers or Dons
Fremantle	the Dockers

Geelong	the Cats or Catters
Gold Coast	the Suns
Greater Western Sydney	the Giants
Hawthorn	the Hawks or Hawkers
Melbourne	the Demons or Dees
North Melbourne	the Kangaroos or Roos
Port Adelaide	Port Power or the Power
Richmond	the Tigers or Tiges
St Kilda	the Saints or Sainters
Sydney	the Swans or Swannies (formerly South Melbourne)
West Coast Eagles	the Eagles
Western Bulldogs	the Dogs or Doggies (formerly Footscray)

The positions

full-back line	two back pockets and one full-back
half-back line	two half-back flanks and one centre half-back
centre line	two wingers
half-forward line	two half-forward flanks and one centre half-forward
full-forward line	two forward pockets and one full-forward
centre square	one ruckman, one ruck rover and two rovers

YA DROP KICK

There are many ways of describing how the ball is kicked, from kicking actions to descriptions of intent or the consequences of a poor kick: **checkside** or **banana kick**; **drop kick** (out of fashion as a kick, but still used as a term of verbal abuse); **drop punt**; **hospital ball**; **lean back and go bang**; **mongrel punt**; **a rain maker**; **screwie**; **set sail for home**; **stab pass**; and a **torpedo** or **torp**.

Major events

The AFL Grand Final takes place on the last Saturday in September at the MCG, and is attended by around 100,000 people and watched on TV by millions.

Another significant AFL event is the televised presentation of the Brownlow Medal, awarded to the player judged best and fairest by the umpires over the whole season. It consists of three hours of vote-counting, and is typically watched only by football addicts and by those who take an active interest in the skimpy outfits worn by footballers' wives and girlfriends.

Rugby league

Traditionally this is the main winter sport in New South Wales and Queensland, although Aussie Rules has made major inroads in the past decade or so, particularly up north due to the success of the Brisbane Lions. 'League' broke away from rugby union in England in the 1890s, many of the rules changed and it rapidly became semiprofessional at the top level. It had spread to Australia (and New Zealand) by 1908 but isn't as well known as rugby union worldwide. The ground (with large H-shaped posts at either end), the ball and the general nature of play are similar to (and in many ways simpler than) union, but most visitors to Australasia will find some details unfamiliar (unless they come from the right part of England!).

There are 13 players on a team (plus **reserves**, ie substitute players). They attempt to get the oval ball past their opponents by handpassing it (always backwards) or kicking it (forwards). Placing the ball on the ground behind the goal line scores a try (four points) which can then be 'converted' by a place kick through the H and over the bar (two more points). There are also penalty goals (two points again) and field goals (one point). A tackled player regains his feet and heels the ball backwards to a colleague, so there's no **rucking** (where players roll the ball with their feet when it's on the ground) or **mauling** (wrestling the ball away from others) as in rugby union – after six tackles the other team gets possession. The opposition can also get possession if the ball goes 'out of play' over the sidelines.

❝ CARN!
– COME ON! ❞

The teams

There are 16 teams in the National Rugby League (NRL), all of which are based on the east coast with the exception of teams from Melbourne and Canberra, and a trans-Tasman team from Auckland.

The positions

Seven backs (one full-back, four three-quarter backs, one five-eighth, one half-back) and six forwards (two props, one hooker, two locks, one loose forward).

Major events

The finals are held in September, culminating in the Grand Final which is held in Sydney. As well, each year New South Wales and Queensland teams are selected to meet in the three 'State of Origin' matches: rugby league at its best. In international rugby league there's a World Cup tournament at which 10 teams play (having first won their qualifying matches), as well as an annual Tri-Nations competition between Australia, New Zealand and Great Britain.

Rugby union

Rugby union is the older code of rugby – in Australia it's often called just 'rugby', in contrast with 'league' – and is better known around the world than rugby league. It was strictly amateur even at the top till the mid-1990s. Until the late 1970s Australia struggled to compete on the international stage, but since then the national team, the Wallabies, have grown to be a dominant force in rugby. They have won the coveted World Cup twice since its inception – the only team to do so.

An international competition called the Super 14 involves regional teams from Australia, New Zealand and South Africa. There's also the Tri Nation Series between these three southern-hemisphere giants of the game.

Rugby union is played 15 a side (eight forwards). Tries are worth five points, conversions two, penalty goals and field goals three. 'Set plays' (preplanned **scrums**, **rucks**, **mauls** and **line-outs**) are more important than in league.

Football (Soccer)

The world game has traditionally been the poor relation of other football codes in Australia, and has historically lacked popular support, being thought of as an immigrant's sport. The main competition, the A-League, is national and is played in the summer. The main catalyst for the sport's growth in the 1990s was the fairly consistent and sometimes excellent form of the national team, the Socceroos, and a growing interest in watching the World Cup. In 2005 the sport was officially rebranded as 'football' in Australia, instead of 'soccer', in an effort to bring it into line with its international peers.

Cricket

Despite various competing attractions, the quintessential Aussie summer sport is still cricket, transplanted from England in colonial times. For those who aren't acquainted with the game, the best way to begin to understand it is to go to a match with someone who's familiar with the rules and can shed light on the arcane proceedings.

One-dayers and **Twenty20** matches – single-day matches in which each side bats once – are very popular, but are regarded by traditionalists as travesties of 'real' Test cricket, which can last four days at state level and five at international level. The **bowler** (pitcher) must 'bowl' the ball at the batsman with a straight arm and not throw it (lest he be branded a **chucker** and the ball called a **no ball**), although fielders can throw it. Six balls (an **over**) are bowled at one of the two sets of stumps, which is defended by one of the two batsmen who are 'in' at any given time. After an over, the whole fielding side (but not the batsmen) change ends and a different bowler bowls the next over at the other set of stumps. This goes on until the innings ends, which usually takes hours (50 to 150 overs).

There are a number of ways the bowler can get a batsman out (which is called **taking a wicket**), the two simplest being to hit the stumps or to induce the batsman to hit the ball up in the air and be caught out. The wicket-keeper behind the stumps is the prime catcher. Batsmen remain at bat until dismissed; when 10 of the 11 in the team are out, the team's **innings** is over (ie the other team takes its turn batting).

Each time the batsmen are able to run past each other and change ends a run is scored. If the ball crosses the boundary the batsman gets four runs, and six runs if it goes over the boundary without touching the ground. Surprising as this may seem to baseball fans, the batsmen aren't required to hit all the balls bowled at them, though missing or ignoring an accurate ball may lead to dismissal by being 'bowled' (having the ball hitting the stumps). If the batsman *does* hit the ball, he doesn't have to run – this is a decision to be made by the two batsmen and depends on the risk of being run out (where the stumps are hit by the ball while a batsman is still out of his **crease**, the painted line at his end of the cricket pitch) and the state of the game. A great score by one batsman would be 100 or more and a top bowler can hope to get five or more of the possible 10 **wickets** (dismissals) in an innings.

BATTLE FOR THE ASHES

One of the sporting world's holiest of holies is a small wooden urn said to contain the ashes of a burnt bail from the 1882 Australia versus England test series. The urn is representative of the 'death' of cricket, said to have occurred as a result of an Australian victory in that series. While its genesis was a bit of a joke, it has since become a great rivalry played out every two years by the two great cricket nations in the Ashes test series.

THE RIVALRY BEGINS

The first international cricket tour of England was in May 1868, by a team of Aboriginal cricketers whose 17 members had already played at the Melbourne Cricket Ground and toured Sydney. In six months they played 47 matches against the English – victorious in 14, defeated in 14 and drawing 19. On return to Australia, the two most outstanding players – Johnny Mullagh and Jimmy Cuzens – were signed up by the Melbourne Cricket Club.

The teams for the main domestic competitions represent the Australian states. The national men's team regularly plays Test, one-day and Twenty20 matches against nine other nations: New Zealand, South Africa, Zimbabwe, Pakistan, India, Bangladesh, Sri Lanka, the West Indies and England. The Australian team has a track record as one of the best in the world.

Women's cricket

Women's cricket in Australia boasts an illustrious history on a par with the Australian men's cricket teams. The first women's team was established in 1874 with a local match in Bendigo, Victoria. The first Test match was played in Brisbane in December 1934, between teams from Australia and England. The women's team first toured England in 1937, New Zealand in 1948–49 and India in 1975.

The Australian women's team competes in an international competition involving 10 other teams and was recently ranked number one in both one-day and Test cricket. It has won four Cricket World Cups (a competition that began in 1973, two years before the introduction of the men's Cricket World Cup).

There are around 27,000 female cricketers playing at school and club levels throughout Australia.

Some Aussie cricket legends

Dennis Lillee

One of the game's finest fast bowlers, adored by Australian crowds in the 1970s and early '80s.

Sir Don Bradman

The greatest batsman ever, garnering an amazing Test average of 99.94 (an average of almost 40 runs per match higher than the next three best batsmen) in a career lasting from 1928 to 1948.

Shane Warne

The greatest leg spin bowler of all time and the game's best wicket-taker at Test level, with 583 and counting. His greatness on the field has been overshadowed by numerous off-field controversies.

....

Surf lifesaving & surfing

Surf lifesaving in Australia started at Manly Beach in Sydney in 1902, when a daring William Gocher broke the law by bathing in daylight. In the years that followed, 'leisure' swimming at beaches became a popular activity and drownings a common occurrence. In response to these dangers of the sea, the New South Wales Surf Bathing Association was formed in 1907, and later became a national body. Its members, who now number over 100,000 in some 280 clubs around the country, have performed hundreds of thousands of rescues, and the national championships attract large crowds. The probability of drowning in Australia is dramatically reduced when swimming between the warning red and yellow flags set up by the Surf Lifesaving Association.

Surfing was first demonstrated to intrigued Australians in 1915, when a Hawaiian called Duke Kahanamoku rode his hand-carved surfboard at Freshwater, on Sydney's north shore. Today,

SLIP, SLOP, SLAP

It doesn't qualify as a sport, but **sunbaking** (sunbathing) has certainly been a national pastime, not just on beaches but also during long cricket matches and other sporting events. Unfortunately, the habit of exposing skin to the blazing Australian sun has given the country one of the world's highest rates of skin cancer. The first and most famous skin cancer awareness campaign, in 1981, urged people to 'Slip, slop, slap – slip on a shirt, slop on sun-cream and slap on a hat'. It and later campaigns have met with varying degrees of success.

local surf beaches are clogged with surfers of all ages waiting for the next swell. Australia boasts several world champions and international surfing events, including the Rip Curl Pro contest (see the box on p100) at Bells Beach in Victoria.

Basketball

Although many people think of basketball as a quintessentially American sport, it has a very respectable participation rate in Australia – around 220,000 men, women and children are registered as playing in some kind of basketball team each year and it's estimated that around 600,000 play in some capacity. Basketball's history in Australia is also surprisingly long. The first game in the country was played in 1905 at the Melbourne YMCA and the sport's governing body, Basketball Australia (then called the Australian Basketball Federation), was founded in 1939. It became a member of FIBA, the International Basketball Federation, as early as 1949.

Today, the main professional competition is the National Basketball League or NBL, with a season that runs from October to April. The parallel women's league, the WNBL, has rather less television coverage.

While the men's national team, the Boomers, isn't quite in the league of teams from nations such as the US or Lithuania, the women's national team, the Opals, has an impressive record and a run of Olympic medals.

Netball

Netball was created by an American basketball coach based in England who set himself a challenge to improve the skills of his charges. This new game was introduced to several schools in England, where it became a popular sport, particularly with women, and quickly spread to Australia. In recent years, Australian teams have been prominent in worldwide netball competitions. Although initially netball was characterised as a female sport, growing interest by men led to the formation of men's and 'mixed' netball teams.

A netball court is approximately the size of a tennis court with a shooting semicircle and goal post at each end. The goal post has no backboard, just a simple hoop for shooting goals – it doesn't, as the name 'netball' may suggest, resemble the netted basket of basketball.

There are 654 netball associations in Australia, and it's estimated that 1.2 million Australians play netball, counting those involved in school, mixed, men's and indoor netball competitions. Netball was introduced as an official sport at the 1998 Commonwealth Games, where the Australian women's team won the gold medal.

SPORT & ENTERTAINMENT

GREAT RACES

Birdsville Races

These races may not get the media coverage of the Melbourne Cup (see p141), but as Australia's premier outback horse race, the Birdsville Races on the first weekend in September are a hugely popular event. And the beer starts flowing early...

Rip Curl Pro

Each Easter weekend, Bells Beach (southwest of Melbourne) attracts top surfers and wannabes to the world's longest-running professional surfing competition.

Sydney to Hobart Yacht Race

For the start of this race on Boxing Day, Sydney Harbour is crammed with hundreds of seacraft from cruisers to dinghies as the competing yachts sail off towards Tasmania. There's a huge street party in Hobart to celebrate the end of this long event.

ENTERTAINMENT

Pubs & clubs

Inner-city pubs and many of their small-town equivalents used to be bastions of live music, where you could go to see Australian bands (usually rock, blues and acoustic/folk outfits) up to several times a week. But in many inner-city areas at least, the stage has been stowed away to make room for poker machines. That said, there are still plenty of hotel venues (particularly in capital cities like Melbourne and Sydney) that frequently host local and international acts. A lot of night – and day – life centres on the pub (especially in country towns). Families come early for a **counter meal**, others linger with mates and a beer or six, play darts or shoot pool (many pubs have pool teams and regular tournaments), or tune into some live rock'n'roll.

> **❝ PUNTER**
> — A CUSTOMER AT A PUB OR BAR **❞**

There are also plenty of clubs in country and suburban areas around which the social life of the community revolves. Such watering holes include sporting clubs, most notably football clubs which have associated football teams and offer extensive drinking and gambling facilities, and RSL (Returned & Services League) clubs, the local chapter of which is sometimes called the **Rozzer**. The other kind of club is a nightclub to which a **punter** (the average person/customer) will go, after kickstarting the night in a bar or cafe – to drink and dance, often until the sun comes up. Australian liquor licensing laws in some areas mean that if you really wanted to you could start out on Friday, get home on Monday, and not stop dancing, drinking or socialising in-between.

Movies, TV & theatre

Australians are ranked among the biggest cinema-goers in the world, with ticket sales increasing every year, and there's no shortage of cinemas and films (**flicks**) for your viewing

HOUSEHOLD NAMES: ENTERTAINERS

Russell Crowe

Technically a Kiwi (New Zealander), but claimed by Australians as their own. An Oscar-winning actor, though also famed for his bad temper and responsible for the underwhelming band 30 Odd Foot of Grunts.

Paul Hogan

Comic actor, previously a Sydney Harbour Bridge worker and then TV comedian. Known for the *Crocodile Dundee* movies and for his ads enticing Americans to visit Australia, including the invitation to 'slip another shrimp on the barbie'.

Barry Humphries

Comedian who has portrayed various quintessentially Australian characters, including Dame Edna Everage and the repulsive Sir Les Patterson.

Nicole Kidman

Hugely successful actor in both mainstream and art-house film roles. She won an Academy Award in 2003 for her portrayal of Virginia Woolf in *The Hours*.

pleasure. Small 'art-house' cinemas show foreign-language and avant-garde films, while large companies like Hoyts and Village compete to show the blockbusters and big names. During the summer months, moonlight cinemas are popular – you can catch a film at night under the stars as you lounge on a picnic blanket or in a deck chair.

Elle Macpherson

Former supermodel and now successful businesswoman, still sometimes referred to by her modelling nickname, 'The Body'.

Ian 'Molly' Meldrum

Since hosting *Countdown*, his epoch-defining music show of the 1970s and '80s, Molly has been an influential fixture of the Australian music scene. Famously never seen without his cowboy hat.

Kylie Minogue

Singer/actor who got her break in the soap opera *Neighbours* and has gone on to become one of the world's top-selling female artists. She was nicknamed the 'Singing Budgie' by critics early in her career.

Bert Newton

Nicknamed 'Moonface', Newton is a very popular and cheesy TV host – one of the originals of Australian television, having been in the limelight since the 1960s.

Australian commercial television is largely dominated by reality TV shows and American and British imports, and re-runs and soap operas like *Neighbours*. Government-sponsored channels the ABC and multicultural SBS provide more worthy, sometimes even educational, fare. All of the country's major cities have thriving arts scenes and even the smallest country towns will have a repertory theatre group.

....

Shopping

> **66** tRACKIE DACKS
> — A FORM OF LEISURE WEAR **99**

In some countries, shopping is what you do when you run out of necessities – but not in Australia, where for many folk shopping is just another way to occupy yourself. Try the following shopping terms on for size:

Akubra	a famous brand of Aussie hat
Australiana	the mass-produced trinkets found in souvenir shops, usually imported from Asia
bumbag	what Americans call a 'fanny pack' (note that in Australia, 'fanny' is vulgar slang for female genitalia, so if you insist on using 'fanny pack' be prepared for either gasps or giggles)
chemist	a pharmacy or pharmacist
clobber	clothes
dacks	trousers; also used to describe tracksuit pants, as in **trackie dacks**

Driza-bone	a famous brand of Aussie oilskin raincoat
haberdashery	a shop that sells sewing supplies
handbag	a woman's carry bag – a 'purse' in North America
hire purchase	what Americans call 'instalment buying'
lay-by	reservation of an item by payment of a deposit – not a roadside stopping place as in the UK
manchester	bed and bathroom linen
moleskins	jeans made of brushed cotton
nappy	known as a 'diaper' by North Americans
pram	a 'baby buggy' in North America
purse	known as a 'change purse' in North America
skivvy	long-sleeved turtleneck top made of stretch cotton
spanner	a 'monkey wrench' in the USA
stroller/pusher	small wheeled chair for small children, often called a 'pushchair' elsewhere
thongs	flip-flops – not skimpy underwear!
vest	a sleeveless outer garment (not a 'singlet' as in the UK)

> **ꞮꞮ** tHONGS
> — FLIP-FLOPS, NOt SKIMPY
> UNDERWEAR! **ꞮꞮ**

Festivals

Here are just a handful of the celebrations which are held around Australia.

Australia Day

On 26 January, Australia commemorates the landing of the First Fleet in 1788 with a national holiday, concerts and other celebrations, and the announcement of the Australia Day Awards, including the award for Australian of the Year. A good occasion for a barbie!

Barunga Festival

Attracting about 40 Aboriginal groups from all over the Northern Territory, this festival in early June is a great way to experience some Aboriginal culture. It's held at Barunga, 80km southeast of Katherine, and has traditional arts and crafts exhibits, native dancing, sports and music. You can sample Australian bush tucker too – honey ants, kangaroo, witchetty (witjuti) grubs and roasted possum, snake and goanna (a lizard).

Beer Can Regatta

This rowdy occasion in July/August is a 'sailing' race at Mindil Beach in Darwin between 'boats' built with empty beer cans – half the fun is emptying the beer cans. For those who prefer activities on terra firma, there are thong-throwing competitions and bathing beauty contests.

Henley-on-Todd Regatta

A boat race on a dry river bed? Head for Alice Springs in August/September to check out the crews 'wearing' their colourful, inventive boat creations as they stir up the dust – bounding for glory down the empty Todd River. And watch out for the Camel

Cup in July when it's the camels' turn (without the seacraft) to compete in the same dry river bed.

Melbourne Moomba Festival

Running over four days in March, this summer festival ends with a street parade reigned over by the year's Moomba Monarch, usually a popular TV or sporting personality. The word moomba was thought to mean 'let's get together and have fun' in an Aboriginal language. In fact, a more accurate translation would be 'up your bum'.

Port Fairy Folk Festival

The usually low-key Victorian coastal town of Port Fairy welcomes a deluge of folk music fans every Labour Day weekend in March. As well as live music, the festival also presents a jam-packed program of storytelling, music classes and singalongs, dancing, a food festival and street markets.

Shinju Matsuri

Around August, the port town of Broome celebrates its pearling history and diverse cultural heritage with Shinju Matsuri (the Pearl Festival). This colourful festival is launched by a traditional opening ball and finishes with a beach concert – Opera-under-the-stars – and a brilliant fireworks display, with must-see dragon boat races in between.

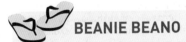

BEANIE BEANO

Alice Springs celebrates the beanie, a popular winter hat, in early July during the Beanie Festival. One of the big drawcards is the competition giving prizes like 'the craziest beanie' and 'the best made beanie'.

Sydney Gay & Lesbian Mardi Gras

Not just a famously spectacular parade and an all-night dance party in Oxford Street, this is a month-long festival in February that also features theatre, art, photography and music in a celebration of gay and lesbian life.

Tamworth Country Music Festival

Yeehah! Tamworth is Australia's 'Country Music Capital' and each January, guitars, voices and award ceremonies entertain the booted throngs for around 10 days. Find a good perch on Peel Street when the cavalcade of floats, bands and line-dancers move through the town for the parade celebrating country music. Rodeos are also a big feature.

Torres Strait Cultural Festival

In September every two years, Thursday Island hosts the Torres Strait Cultural Festival, designed to promote and strengthen the islands' cultural identity. Activities include traditional dance, traditional and contemporary singing, and stalls selling food, handicraft and carvings.

B & S BALLS

Bachelors' & Spinsters' Balls – held in big tents and shearing sheds in rural areas all over Australia – attract the young and thirsty in their thousands. Alcohol is **skolled** in mind-blowing amounts by bachelors in black tie and spinsters in taffeta gowns.

Royal shows

Each capital city has a royal show offering livestock contests, agricultural displays, novelty rides and sideshows. The cake-decorating competitions and the showing-off of primped and preened cats and dogs also (amazingly) draw people by the thousands. Kids find the 'showbags' containing chocolate, lollies, toys and other wares hard to resist. This is the place to gobble down fairy floss, toffee apples and dagwood dogs.

March/April	Royal Easter Show, Sydney
July	Royal Darwin Show, NT
August	Royal National Agricultural Show (the Ekka), Brisbane
August/ September	Royal Shows, Melbourne, Adelaide, Perth

❝ DAGWOOD DOG
— DEEP-FRIED, BATTERED-SAUSAGE
GOODNESS ❞

Film festivals

Celebrations of celluloid are held in each major city and showcase contemporary films from around Australia and the globe. The International Film Festival in Melbourne has long been regarded as Australia's best, offering film buffs fabulous cinema during the winter months of July and August. Short film festivals are also popular – check out Tropfest in Sydney or the St Kilda Film Festival in Melbourne.

Arts festivals

There are various arts festivals staged around Australia that act as magnets for 'culture vultures' and give thousands of local and international artists an opportunity to wow audiences with their talents. On offer is an extraordinary range of opera, dance, drama, comedy, film, music, visual arts, literature and street parades, interspersed with plenty of parties.

Sydney Festival (January)   kickstarted by a fireworks extravaganza above the Harbour Bridge on New Year's Eve

Perth International Arts Festival (February/March) the oldest, and one of the largest, of the arts festivals

Adelaide Festival of Arts (March)   considered by many to be the most innovative of all the arts festivals. There's also an excellent 'alternative' festival called **Adelaide Fringe**.

Brisbane Riverfestival (September)   Brisbane's major festival of the arts, with buskers, concerts and other performances

Melbourne Festival (October)   combines big-name Australian and international performers and visual artists. It's preceded in September by the **Melbourne Fringe Festival**, which focuses on new and 'innovative' art.

 **DESERT MOB**

Every September the Desert Mob art show at the Araluen Centre in Alice Springs exhibits a diverse range of work from established and emerging Aboriginal artists from all over the Northern Territory, South Australia and Western Australia.

Gambling

Australians appear to be addicted to gambling and are likely to bet on just about anything, including the likelihood of whether or not they'll bet on anything. One of the most popular forms of gambling is the coin-operated device that elsewhere is known as a 'slot machine' but here is called a 'poker machine', **pokie** or **one-armed bandit**. These machines used to be restricted to casinos and social clubs but nowadays have swamped many pubs as well.

Long before the advent of the poker machine, however, there was the game of **two-up**. A person known as the **spinner** – summoned into the middle of a ring with the call 'Come in spinner' – would hold a flat board called a **paddle** or **kip** on which two coins rested. The spinner would toss the coins into the air and gamblers would bet on whether the coins would land showing two heads or two tails – if the coins showed one head and one tail it would be deemed an **odd toss** and no money would be won or lost. The game is rarely seen nowadays, though some casinos still stage it.

Taking a punt (betting) on the **nags** or the **gee-gees** (the horses) is probably the most popular form of gambling in Australia, particularly when horse racing carnivals or major events such as the Melbourne Cup (see p141) are being held. Nowhere near as high profile as horse racing but still popular are the **dogs** (greyhound racing).

A more discreet form of gambling takes place in news-agents which sell **scratchies** – lottery tickets that have panels you scratch off with a coin to potentially reveal a prize underneath.

Would you take a Captain Cook at that!

SLANG &
MISUNDERSTANDINGS

SLANG & MISUNDERSTANDINGS

Look out for these...

CLASSIC PHRASE:
SHE'LL BE APPLES
Everything will be okay

TRY THIS ONE:
REGGIES
Most Aussies these days would be bamboozled by this rhyming slang for underwear (Reg Grundies = undies)

USE WITH CAUTION:
WOG
Though originally a derogatory term for Mediterranean immigrants, they have largely reclaimed it for themselves and commonly use it with pride

MISUNDERSTANDINGS:
CROOK
Might mean variously that you're angry, feeling sick in the stomach or a criminal

SLANG & MISUNDERSTANDINGS

If you're a visitor to Australia, you may be puzzled by hearing a red-headed person nicknamed Blue or Bluey. Then there's feeling blue meaning 'feeling depressed', making a blue meaning 'making a mistake', picking a blue meaning 'starting a fight or argument', watching a blue movie meaning 'watching a pornographic film' and the boys in blue meaning 'the police'.

The word crook is another minefield – there's feeling crook meaning 'feeling sick', eating something crook meaning 'eating something likely to cause food poisoning', being crook at/with someone meaning 'being angry with them', being a crook meaning 'being a swindler or a thief' and something being crook meaning 'something being illegal or broken'.

Confused? Welcome to the Australian colloquialism.

> **CHUCK A BERKO – EXPRESS EXTREME ANGER**

Doing things

bag	criticise
bludge	laze around, evade responsibilities
bored shitless	be extremely bored
bung	put, as in 'Just bung it in the oven'
cark it	collapse or die
chuck a berko	express extreme anger

come a cropper	fall over, have an accident or fail
cream	defeat decisively
dip your lid	show respect for someone or something
fart-arse around	waste time
feel like a shag on a rock	feel alone, deserted, forlorn, left out
front up	present yourself, make an appearance
get a guernsey	succeed or win approval (originally to be selected for a football team – a guernsey is a football jumper)
get stuck into somebody	criticise someone

FART-ARSE AROUND
– WASTE TIME

give a bum-steer	mislead someone
give it a burl	try
hang out for	anticipate eagerly
have a lash at it	try
have a shot at it	try
have tickets on yourself	have an inflated opinion of your own worth
live on the smell of an oily rag	live frugally
muck around	fool around
pick the eyes out of it	take all the best bits

play funny buggers	be silly or behave dishonestly
pull a swiftie	do something dishonest or unfair
pull your head in	mind your own business
rapt	enthusiastic or happy (enraptured)
rubbish (someone)	pour scorn on
see a man about a dog	do something secretively – usually going to the toilet
shoot through	die or leave (quickly)
skite	boast
spill your guts	reveal a secret or your feelings
stick your bib in	interfere
stir the possum	tease and/or deliberately cause trouble
strike a blow	help with something (eg housework)
swing the billy	put the kettle on with the intention of making a cup of tea
tee up	arrange something (eg a meeting)
wag	skip school without permission

❝ PLAY FUNNY BUGGERS
— BE SILLY ❞

People

Someone who **couldn't organise a piss-up in a brewery** is very disorganised, but if there are **no flies on him/her** the person is clever, alert and can't easily be fooled. Others **would come to the opening of an envelope** (that is, they're social climbers and/or party addicts who will come to any party or function), but **wouldn't shout if a shark bit them** (are too stingy to buy drinks for others). And some people you just **don't know from a bar of soap** – you've never met them before.

People can also be described as being **born in a tent** (having a tendency to leave doors open), being **lower than a snake's belly/armpits** (very mean, cruel or dishonest), being **rough as guts** (very rough, uncivilised or rude) or being **rooted**, **stuffed** or **zonked** (exhausted). Here are some more terms:

anklebiter	child
bloke	man – but the American terms 'guy' and 'dude' are often used instead
blow-in	unexpected or uninvited guest
bludger	someone who does no or very little work
blue heeler	police officer (from the name of a breed of Australian cattle dog)
bogan	someone (usually working-class and urban) considered to lack style and sophistication
checkout chick	supermarket checkout clerk
curly	nickname for a bald person
fruit loop	silly or crazy person ('fruit loops' are a sugary breakfast cereal)
hoon	a young man who drives fast and/or recklessly

Joe Blow/Bloggs	the average citizen, any man
larrikin	either a cheeky and irreverent person or a lout (old-fashioned)
mate	friend
no-hoper	a loser, someone very incompetent
old cheese	mother
poofter	homosexual man (offensive)
quack	doctor (can be contemptuous)
rug rat	child
shitkicker	someone who does all the menial or unpopular jobs
tacker	child
tight-arse	stingy person
wally	fool, idiot
wanker	idiot and/or someone pretentious

Places & things

You might have **more of something than you could poke a stick at** (a lot of it) in which case you'd probably be happy to give it away. On the other hand, if you would like something returned, tell the borrower it's a **boomerang**!

> **❝ DOOVELACKI. THINGAMA-JIG. WHATCHAMACALLIt**
> — A THING **❞**

Places or things can also be:

ace	good
all the go	fashionable
as scarce as hen's teeth	very rare
cactus	broken or useless
cheap as chips	very cheap
chock-a-block	completely full
chockers	full (from 'chock-a-block')
cruddy	poor quality
grouse	good
not worth a brass razoo	not worth anything
not worth a crumpet	worthless
on the nose	very smelly
o.s.	overseas
a ripoff	overpriced
skewiff	askew
squiffy	askew or tipsy
wonky	unstable, unsteady

Here are a few other colloquialisms you might be puzzled by:

blower	telephone
idiot box	television
pong	bad smell
poo tickets	toilet paper
shrapnel	small-denomination coins
thingo	a thing; also a **doovelacki**, **thingamajig** or **whatchamacallit**

Actions & situations

Aussie salute	the action of brushing flies away from your face
belter	really good, as in 'It was a belter'
bingle	car accident
blind Freddy	used to point out how obvious something is, as in 'Even blind Freddy would see that'
cooking with gas	something going well and as planned
crust	a living, as in 'What do you do for a crust?'
dead cert/set	absolutely certain
fizzer	a failure, disappointment, as in 'The party was a real fizzer'
flat chat/out	doing something very quickly
flat out like a lizard drinking	very busy
get a wriggle on	hurry up
hang on a tick/sec	wait a moment
in strife	in difficulties (not necessarily arguing or fighting)
in two shakes of a lamb's tail	in a very short amount of time
not even in the race for it	having no hope of achieving a goal
piece of piss	easy task
playing pocket billiards	man adjusting his genitals
prang	car accident
Rafferty's rules	no rules at all, very disorganised

SLANG & MISUNDERSTANDINGS

Rattle your dags!	Hurry up!
Reckon!	You bet!
ron	later (a contraction of 'later on')
r.s.	lousy (short for 'ratshit')
rug up	dress warmly
she'll be apples	everything will be okay
she's sweet	as for **she'll be apples**
spewing	literally, vomiting – but often used to mean 'upset' or 'disappointed'
stinker	a very hot day
Too right!	yes, most definitely, of course
wog	virus or stomach upset; derogatory term for someone of Mediterranean extraction
yonks	a long time, as in 'I haven't seen Thommo for yonks'

BUCKLEY'S, MATE!

If somebody tells you that you have **Buckley's**, **Buckley's chance** or **Buckley's and none**, they're saying you have little or no chance. This expression refers in part to convict William Buckley, who managed to escape from the Port Phillip Bay penal colony in 1803 and was considered to have no chance of surviving. (In fact, he ended up living with the Aboriginal people of the present-day Geelong area for over 30 years before being rediscovered by the authorities.) The expression only became fully formed after Buckley's chance became tied to a pun on the name of a Melbourne department store which opened in 1851, Buckley and Nunn – hence, Buckley's and none.

Like a dunny in a desert

The little expression 'like a...' opens a world of possibilities in Australian slang. A few of the more well-known or remarkable comparisons follow.

like a cocky on a biscuit tin left out, not included. Used after Arnotts chose a colourful parrot rather than a sulphur-crested cockatoo to become part of their logo.

like a dunny in a desert standing out, very conspicuous

like a moll at a christening extremely out of place and uncomfortable

like a rat up a drain pipe very quick, restless and erratic

like a rooster one day and a feather duster the next very important, special and useful one moment and very unimportant and common the next

like a stunned mullet in a state of complete confusion, astonishment or inertia. The mullet, being a large fish, is knocked over the head after it's been caught, and as it's a common fish to catch perhaps its dazed expression has become familiar.

Other 'like a...' expressions include:

built like a brick shithouse a large solidly built person, usually a man

charge like a wounded bull charge outrageously high prices

feel like a grease spot feel hot and sweaty

go down like a lead balloon be a complete failure

go through (someone) like a dose of salts have a laxative effect. Of a person, be very angry with someone.

looks like a dog's breakfast is in a dreadful mess

need (something) like a hole in the head don't need it at all

running around like a headless chook making a lot of commotion but not getting anywhere. It refers to a **chook** (chicken) intended for the day's dinner getting its head cut off – sometimes the headless chook runs around until the message finally gets through to its body that it's dead.

Feelings & descriptions

Here's where we get some really creative, if not downright bizarre, and sometimes hilarious, imagery.

Crudeness
rough as a goat's knees
rough as a pig's breakfast
rough as bags

Dryness
dry as a bone
dry as a chip
dry as a dead dingo's donger
dry as a nun's nasty
dry as a Pommy's towel

Fitness
fit as a Mallee bull

Fullness
full as a boot
full as a bull's bum
full as a footy final
full as a goog (ie an egg)
full as a state school hat rack
full as a tick
full to pussy's bow

❝ USEFUL AS TITS ON A BULL
— NOT VERY USEFUL ❞

Happiness
happy as a dog with two tails
happy as Larry

Insanity
has a few roos loose in the top paddock
mad as a cut snake
mad as a frilled lizard
mad as a gumtree full of galahs
mad as a maggot
mad as a meataxe
mad as a mother-in-law's cat
off your rocker
off your scone
silly as a bagful of worms
silly as a wheel

Sadness
happy as a bastard on Father's Day
miserable as a bandicoot
miserable as a shag on a rock

Uselessness
useful as a glass door on a dunny
useful as a hip pocket on a singlet
useful as a sore arse to a boundary rider
useful as a third armpit
useful as tits on a bull

Weakness

weak as piss

weak as water

weaker than a sunburned snowflake

A snag short of a barbie

Australians often use 'short of a...' phrases to talk about someone who seems a bit stupid or mentally unstable. Occasionally you might hear someone described as:

a book short of a library	a can short of a slab
an egg short of a dozen	a grape short of a bunch
a penny short of a pound	a sandwich short of a picnic
a snag short of a barbie	a stubby short of a sixpack

Rhyming slang

Rhyming slang was borrowed from Cockney English, and then added to in Australia. Some, always older, Australians seem to enjoy using it to spice up their conversation, but it doesn't form a large part of everyday speech. It's still funny though.

after darks	sharks
aristotle	bottle
babbling brook	cook
Bob Hope	soap
Captain Cook	look
cheese and kisses	missus (wife)
comic cuts	guts
dead horse	sauce, usually tomato sauce

dog and bone	phone
hammer and tack	back
hey-diddle-diddle	piddle
hit-and-miss	piss
Jimmy Britts	shits
Jimmy Dancer	cancer
Joe Blake	snake
Noah's ark	shark
on one's Pat Malone	alone
optic nerve	perve (look)
Richard the Third	turd
steak and kidney	Sydney
tom(my) tits	shits

> **A SNAG SHORt OF A BARBIE**
> — NOt VERY SMARt

amster – Amsterdam ram
an old-fashioned word for a person who tries to drum up business outside a sideshow. 'Amsterdam ram' is a British word for the same kind of showman, also known as a **drummer**, **spruiker** or **urger**.

barmaid's blush – a flush (in poker)
also refers to a drink made from port wine and lemonade, or rum and raspberry

Barry Crocker – a shocker
a poor performance

ME OLD COBBER!

The word **cobber**, an old-fashioned Aussie word for 'friend', stems from 'to cob' meaning 'to take a liking to someone', originally from a Suffolk dialect of the 1800s.

butcher's (hook) – crook
feeling sick. When you have the **lurgy** (some vague unidentifiable illness, usually one that's going around), then you 'feel butcher's'. Not to be confused with the below.

butcher's (hook) – look
as in 'Have a butcher's at this'

china (plate) – mate
old-fashioned word for a friend

Dad and Dave – shave
'Dad and Dave' was a well-known radio show during the 1930s, '40s and '50s

frog and toad – road
as in 'Let's hit the frog'n'toad!'

loaf (of bread) – head
'use your loaf' is an encouragement to think

onka(paringa) – finger
Onkaparinga is also the name of a brand of woollen blanket

reginalds (Reg Grundies) – undies
underwear. Reg Grundy was a well-known TV entrepreneur. **Reginalds** are also known as **reggies**.

scarper (Scapa Flow) – go
go away, usually at high speed or with some urgency

septic (tank) – Yank
an American. Also shortened to **seppo**.

titfer (tit for tat) – hat
another term for hat is **this-an'-that**

warwick (Warwick Farm) – arm
named after a well-known racecourse in Sydney

···

Misunderstandings

Despite the spirit of sharing that exists between Australian English and other forms of English, there are numerous instances of disagreement over which word to use. Following are some of the most common examples.

American English

Australian English	American English
barrack for	root for
bonnet	car hood
boot	trunk
braces (for trousers)	suspenders
camp bed	cot
capsicum	(bell) pepper
cot	crib
cyclone	hurricane
fairy floss	candy floss
fringe (hair)	bangs
ground floor	1st floor
lollies	candy

takeaway	takeout
torch	flashlight
university	college

❝ SEPtIC
— AN AMERICAN ❞

British English

Australian English	British English
bank teller	cashier
bushwalking	walking/hiking
doona	duvet
eggplant	aubergine
freeway	motorway
garbo	dustman
highway	dual carriageway
icy pole/iceblock	(ice) lolly
lollies	sweets
overseas	abroad
paddock	field
private school	public school
public holiday	bank holiday
wharfie	docker
windcheater	sweatshirt
zucchini	courgette

STICKY BEAKS & BASHED EARS

To have a gander doesn't mean 'to eat a goose', it means 'to look at' and so do these phrases:

bo-peep	'Take a bo-peep at that bloke'
geezer	'Ey, have a geezer at that'
perve	to look at lustfully
squizz	'Hey, cop a squizz at this!'
sticky beak	to look, usually uninvited, as in 'I had a sticky beak at the neighbour's new pool when they were out'

There are also quite a few ways to describe incessant talk, including:

chew someone's ear off	ear bash
flap the gums	have a chinwag
raving on	talk someone blind
talk the leg off a chair	verbal diarrhoea
yacking	yapping

New Zealand English

Australian English	New Zealand English
abattoir/slaughterhouse	freezing works
bitumen road	tarseal road
bushwalking	tramping
doona	duvet
esky	coolie bin

gravel/dirt road	metal road
holiday home	bach/crib (mainly Otago)
milk bar	dairy
speed humps/bumps	judder bars
thongs/sandals	jandals
uni	varsity (still heard in the UK as well, but mainly for Oxford and Cambridge)

Black spider

Lime spider

REGIONAL VARIATIONS

Look out for these...

CLASSIC PHRASE:
MORE FRONT THAN MYER

Meaning brazen or cheeky, this phrase originates from a Melbourne department store

TRY THIS ONE:
SPIDER

In southeastern states, it's an ice-cream soda – yum!

USE WITH CAUTION:
BANANABENDERS

Insulting term for Queenslanders used by people of other states. And Tasmanians supposedly have two heads.

MISUNDERSTANDINGS:
CHEERIOS, SAVELOYS, LITTLE BOYS

They're all names for cocktail frankfurts

REGIONAL VARIATIONS

There are two schools of thought about linguistic variations in Australia. One school suggests that different regional dialects are emerging, the other says that Australian English is generally the same across the country. Both schools are partly right. There's increasing evidence of regional differences, but compared to other English-speaking countries these are few and minor. This might seem surprising considering the large distances between most Australian cities, but the country was settled mainly along the coast within a rather short period and the mix of origins in the various cities was apparently fairly similar.

The most obvious regional differences involve vocabulary, and even those who stress linguistic uniformity admit there are quite a few of these. The regionalists, however, claim difference not just in the words we use but also in the way they are pronounced. It's claimed that a Melburnian can be distinguished from a Sydneysider, that everyone can tell a Queenslander, and that the South Australians can be picked as soon as they say 'school'. There are indeed differences in pronunciation (for more on pronunciation see p23) but like most of the vocabulary differences these mainly involve tendencies rather than absolute contrasts. The differences are nowhere near as major as those which separate an Australian from a New Zealander, who simply has to ask for 'fush and chups' to be identified and whose English is travelling further along its own track with each generation.

The table on p138 gives a few of the terms which differ from state to state.

New South Wales

New South Welshmen have sometimes been called **cornstalks**. It seems that quite early in colonial days the climate and way of life agreed with the newcomers, and the men who grew up in Australia became noted for their height and slim build. They grew like cornstalks, with the body characteristically tapering from broad shoulders to slim hips.

> **❝ UP A GUM tREE**
> — CONFUSED **❞**

About Sydney

The capital city of New South Wales has the Harbour Bridge, the Opera House, one of the world's finest harbours and a generally hedonistic climate. This leads some Sydneysiders to believe that Sydney is 'where it's at' and that all other Australian cities are urban irrelevancies. This point of view is of particular irritation to some Melburnians, mainly because said Melburnians believe that *their* city is the hub of Australian life. The parochialism of both cities tends to annoy everyone else in the country.

Sydney was named after Thomas Townshend, 1st Viscount Sydney, by Governor Arthur Phillip (1738–1814), the British naval officer who brought the First Fleet to Sydney Cove. Townshend was Secretary of the Home Department at the time.

As well as naming the city, Governor Phillip is the first person to have recorded the term **gum tree** for a eucalypt in his journal of 1789. The name was considered apt because the substance oozing from the tree was thought to be a kind of gum. Fifty years later it's clear that the colony had not only identified gum trees but knew what it was like to be up them. In the Australian context, **up a gum tree** came to mean 'in a state of confusion' or 'in a hopeless predicament' (a reference to the state of an animal trapped up a tree). The first recorded example of the phrase was a settler commenting on the behaviour of his workforce: 'My convicts were always drinking rum, I often wished they were up a gum tree.' (Some would say workplace relations in Australia have struggled to rise from this low point.)

New South Wales lingo

the Coathanger   an irreverent name for the Harbour Bridge

Pitt Street farmer   a city businessman who channels money into country property – he stereotypically wears a suit during the week and moleskins and workboots on the weekends

shoot through like a Bondi tram   when Sydney had trams, there was one that went to Bondi Beach. Apparently there was a stretch of the track near Centennial Park when the tram picked up speed. Nowadays, to shoot through like a Bondi tram is basically to leave very quickly.

up the Cross   if Bondi Beach represents everything that's fine in life, then King's Cross stands for everything that's sinful. These days it's a little outclassed by Oxford Street, but to go up the Cross is still to enter a gritty, down-at-heel world.

ROSELLA JAM

A woman moved from Queensland, where a **rosella** is a type of fruit, to northern New South Wales, where it's a type of bird. She asked a local if he could get her some rosellas, and he enquired whether two would suffice – he was understandably surprised when she said she'd need more, as she wanted to make jam!

REGIONAL VARIATIONS

DIFFERENT STANDARDS

While there may be many Perth dwellers who have never called a swimming costume 'bathers' (for example), the following terms are generally typical of the different states:

NSW	QLD	SA
10oz glass of beer		
middy	middy	schooner
children's playground equipment for sliding down		
slippery dip; slide	slippery dip	slippery dip; slide
a common black-and-white bird		
magpie; peewee	magpie; peewee	Murray magpie; peewee
costume worn when swimming		
cozzie; togs	togs	bathers; togs
fizzy drink with a dollop of ice cream		
ice-cream soda	ice-cream soda	spider
mid-morning break at primary school		
playlunch; recess	little lunch; recess	playtime
non-alcoholic carbonated sweet drink		
soft drink	cordial	soft drink
round slice of potato covered in batter and deep-fried		
potato scallop	potato scallop	potato fritter
rubber loop used to hold small objects together		
rubber band	rubber band	lacky band
small red sausages at cocktail parties		
cocktail frankfurts	cheerios	frankfurts

TAS	VIC	WA
pot	pot	pot
slide	slide	slippery dip
magpie; mudlark	magpie; mudlark	magpie
bathers; togs	bathers; togs	bathers; togs
spider	spider	ice-cream soda
playtime	playlunch	recess
cordial	soft drink	soft drink
potato cake	potato cake	potato cake
rubber band	lacker band	rubber band
saveloys; little boys	cocktail sausages	frankfurts

Victoria

Victoria was once known as **the Cabbage Garden** because of the state's early ability to produce fruit and vegetables from its rich soil and accommodating climate. Victorians therefore were referred to as **Cabbage Gardeners**, the implication being that that's all they were good for. Victorians are also described as **Mexicans**, because from the point of view of New South Wales they are 'south of the border'.

About Melbourne

Victoria's capital, Melbourne was named in 1837 by Governor Bourke after Lord Melbourne, the British prime minister at the time. Melbourne is more English in its appearance than any other Australian capital, and its residents claim to live stylishly – to dine and dress well, and to be as cultured and sophisticated as Sydney is flamboyant.

One of Melbourne's distinctive features is its trams. They provide a pleasant way to move around the city, although it can be a slow ride to the suburbs.

Victorian lingo

like Bourke Street   very busy, usually referring to traffic. Bourke Street is one of the busiest thoroughfares in Melbourne's central business district.

City Loop   the collective name for the five train stations arranged around the edge of the CBD

has more front than Myer   is cheeky, not at all shy. Myer is a department store that originated in Melbourne.

hook turn   a driving manoeuvre which is only done in Melbourne's CBD and terrifies the rest of Australia. To turn right at an intersection, a motorist pulls over to the left of the road and then crosses all lanes of traffic to complete

AT THE RACES

The Melbourne Cup, the country's biggest horse race, still brings the nation to an almost eerie halt on the first Tuesday of each November to watch the 3.2km race (and an actual halt in Melbourne where it's the excuse for a public holiday). Held at Flemington Racecourse since 1861, the meeting draws a mix of elegantly turned out society types and boisterous masses enjoying the chance to dress up and get **hammered** (drunk) in the car park. Most of the rest of the country joins Cup sweeps, choosing a horse at random and placing a bet for possibly the only time of the year. It's rare to find an Aussie, especially a Melburnian, who isn't having a **flutter** (bet) on the horses on this day.

the turn. The hook turn is designed to keep the tram tracks clear of cars waiting to turn.

the Tan   a popular 4km jogging track around Kings Domain and the Royal Botanic Gardens

....

Queensland

Nicknamed 'the Sunshine State', Queensland certainly has more than its fair share of warm rays, and its coast attracts holidaymakers from all over Australia. However, inland Queensland, stretching up towards Cape York, is as tough a strip of outback as you could encounter. Towards the north is a region called the Channel Country in which numerous interlocking rivers regularly flood to form an inland sea.

Queensland is known as **Bananaland** and its inhabitants as **Bananabenders**, because of the big banana plantations on its southeastern coast.

About Brisbane

Brisbane, Queensland's capital, was established as a convict settlement for the worst offenders, and was celebrated in song as a place of ultimate despair. The city was named after Sir Thomas Brisbane, who was governor of New South Wales from 1821 to 1825. Notwithstanding this grim past, it has a reputation as a rather hedonistic city – steamy in summer but with a beautiful, clear, sunny winter to compensate.

Queensland lingo

duchess dressing table

the Gabba the Brisbane Cricket Ground, so called because of its location in the suburb of Woolloongabba

port a suitcase – short for 'portmanteau'

Schoolies' Week the rowdy end-of-year festivities for high school graduates after their final exams, usually centred on the Gold Coast

windsor sausage a type of processed meat, sold as **devon**, **fritz** and **polony** in other states

....

Australian Capital Territory

The Australian Capital Territory is the small area of land surrounding the country's capital, Canberra.

❝ CROWEATERS
— PEOPLE FROM SOUTH AUSTRALIA ❞

About Canberra

Canberra has the feel of a big country town. It's a unique blend of town, gown (ie academia) and public service, full of politicians who zap in for the season in Parliament, and zap out again as fast as their planes can carry them.

The name 'Canberra' is thought to be the Aboriginal name for the area, meaning something like 'meeting place'. The American architect Walter Burley Griffin (1876–1937) created the original design of the city, and people are still divided about it. Almost everyone says they immediately get lost in Canberra's many roundabouts. (Those spending weary hours attempting to escape the endless loops and whirls have been known to hurl abuse at Griffin!)

ACT lingo

bush week   the name for end-of-term student celebrations at the Australian National University

govie/guvvie home   a government-funded residence, usually offering low rent. An **ex-govie** is one of these residences being offered on the open market.

govie/guvvie school   a government-funded school (**state school** elsewhere)

South Australia

There are a lot of wide open spaces in South Australia – 1% of the population inhabits a whopping 80% of the state's land. As well as being home to some of Australia's leading wine districts, South Australia can claim to be the only Australian colony never to have admitted convicts.

South Australians are occasionally known as **Croweaters** – supposedly because life was so hard in the state that the colonials would be forced to eat crows.

About Adelaide

South Australia's capital is a pleasant town, well-heeled and respectable, as easy to live in as a country town and as interesting as an international city. It's named after Queen Adelaide, the wife of William IV, and is also known as the **City of Churches**. Its biggest claim to fame is probably the Adelaide Festival of Arts, an annual affair which draws local and international talent.

South Australian lingo

donkey   to give someone a ride on the back of your bike, what other Australians would refer to as either a **dink** or a **dinky**

fritz   also known as **bung fritz**, this is the South Australian word for **devon** – processed sandwich meat. It's a German term, brought to the state by the strong German community near Adelaide.

Stobie pole   kind of telegraph pole made of concrete and steel, named after its creator, JC Stobie

....

Northern Territory

The inhabitants of the Northern Territory are known as **Territorians**, naturally enough, or **Top Enders**.

About Darwin

Darwin, the capital, was named after Charles Darwin, the English naturalist, who visited Australia aboard HMS *Beagle* in 1836. Darwin has always been a multicultural city, funnelling traffic between the islands and peninsulas of Asia to Australia's Top End. One result of this is some excellent Asian food markets, particularly on Mindil Beach, which meant that Darwin folk were eating laksa (Chinese-Malay noodle soup) for years before it appeared on menus in Sydney and Melbourne.

Northern Territory lingo

the Wet   the monsoon season

the Dry   the opposite of the Wet. The final stage of this is referred to as **the build-up** (to the Wet) and is notorious for causing great irritability among inhabitants.

Darwin rig or **Territory rig**   a style of casual dress for men that's suitable for the humid conditions of the Top End, usually a short-sleeved, open-neck shirt and trousers

Territory formal   means a long-sleeved shirt and tie – no jacket required. These terms are often written at the bottom of invitations.

> **❝ tERRItORY FORMAL**
> **— tOP END DRESS CODE ❞**

....

Tasmania

Tasmanians feel they are often overlooked by the rest of Australia – which they refer to as **the Mainland**, the inhabitants being **Mainlanders**. And certainly something seems to get lost in the translation over Bass Strait, so that Tasmania and the rest of Australia are never quite on the same wavelength.

Tasmania is also called the **Apple Isle**, a name that refers to the island's past success in growing apples; the inhabitants are sometimes referred to as **Apple Islanders**. **Tassie** is an affectionate shortening of the name Tasmania, while **Taswegian** is a common name for a Tasmanian.

About Hobart

Tasmania's capital is the second oldest city in Australia – the second convict settlement was established there in 1804. The city has an old-world charm: a fishing village character marked by docks and Georgian houses, with Mt Wellington towering above it. It was named after Robert Hobart, fourth Earl of Buckinghamshire and Secretary of State for War and the Colonies (1801-04). A rivalry exists between Hobart and Launceston which is similar to the tension between Sydney and Melbourne. Whatever Hobart does, Launceston has to equal or do better.

Tasmanian lingo

chalet   an outhouse or small dwelling in the garden of a house

mutton bird   a species of shearwater which nests on islands off Tasmania and is considered a gourmet meal, though it's extremely oily

Western Australia

Western Australia is Australia's largest state, encompassing extremes of landscape and weather. As a result words like 'remote' and 'isolated' turn up everywhere, as in the terms **isolated child**, **isolated class**, **isolated school** and **isolated pharmacy**, or **remote posting**, **remote resident** and **remote site**.

Western Australians are sometimes called **Sandgropers**, because most of the state is desert. (To 'sandgrope' is to walk in soft sand, a procedure that most people find tiring.) Sandgroper can be shortened to **Groper** – and Gropers, of course, live in **Groperland**. The state is also sometimes referred to as **Westralia**, so Western Australians are also **Westralians**.

About Perth

Perth is separated from Australia's southern states by the Nullarbor Plain (**Nullarbor** being derived from the Latin 'nulla arbor', meaning 'no tree'). It was named by Captain James Stirling after the city of the same name in Scotland.

On the whole, people in this remote city show few signs of feeling far removed from the more populated bits of the country, and seem content with the beautiful city they have. Western Australians – who from time to time are heard to mutter about secession – refer to inhabitants of the east coast as **t'othersiders** and **Eastern Staters**.

Western Australian lingo

the doctor   the cool sea breeze which blows inland in the late afternoon. In Perth it's known as the **Fremantle doctor** because it blows into Perth from the direction of Fremantle.

Kal   what the locals call Kalgoorlie

Nyungar   a Western Australian Aborigine. In a local Aboriginal language **nyungar** means 'man'.

Rotto   Rottnest Island

skimpy   a scantily clad barmaid

QUOKKAS

Alarmed by the number of what appeared to be huge rats on a sandy island 19km off the Western Australian coast, the Dutch explorer De Vlamingh named the island in their honour – Rottnest, literally 'Rat's Nest'. The animals weren't rats, of course, but the very cute **quokkas**, relatives of the wallaby.

Other regions

Although they're not states or territories, a few other regions in Australia have distinct identities – the Riverina, New England and the Gold Coast.

The Riverina (& Sunraysia)

The lifeline of the Riverina is the Murray River, which feeds off the waters from the Snowy Mountains and then flows all the way to St Vincent's Gulf in South Australia. The area known as Sunraysia is centred on Mildura, Victoria, and sprang up around an irrigation scheme developed in 1923 which made the dried fruit and wine industries of the region possible.

New England

New England, northeast of Sydney, is the district which claims the university town of Armidale as its centre. It's a farming and mining district – the name 'New England' has to be seen as wishful thinking on the part of the settlers.

The Gold Coast

The strip of coastline just south of Brisbane is known as the Gold Coast. It's a tourist phenomenon – high-rises perched on the edge of the beach. Other sections of the coast have also been given names, including the Sunshine Coast (further north) and the Capricorn Coast (the coastline near Rockhampton).

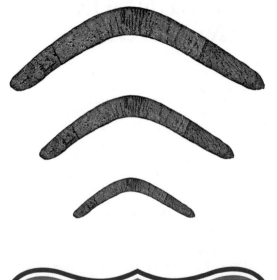

INDIGENOUS
LANGUAGES

INDIGENOUS LANGUAGES

The original inhabitants of Australia have been living on this continent for something like 50,000 years. When the British established the first European settlement in Australia at Sydney Cove in 1788, the newcomers originally called the older inhabitants 'natives' and later 'Aborigines' or 'Aboriginal people'. Recently the term 'Indigenous' has come into general use to replace 'Aboriginal'. Some Aboriginal people prefer to use one of their own names for themselves, which differ from area to area. There's no indigenous term that covers all Aboriginal people – the term **Murri** is used in Queensland, **Nyungar** (or **Nyoongah** or **Noongar**) in the southwest of Western Australia, **Yolŋu** in northeastern Arnhem Land, **Koori** or **Koorie** in New South Wales and Victoria, and **Palawa** in Tasmania.

The size of the Aboriginal population at the time the first Europeans came to Australia is not known, but estimates range from 300,000 to over a million. The people were hunter-gatherers – that is, they lived by hunting animals and gathering various plant foods. Each person belonged to a land-owning group, typically a clan with its own distinctive speech. Often a group of neighbouring clans would have similar forms of speech and we could say that these clans spoke dialects of a particular language.

It's estimated that in 1788 there were about 250 different languages in Australia, each comprising several dialects. However, over the course of the next 100 years the British took over the whole of Australia and in the process many Aboriginal people died, either as a result of introduced diseases or through being deliberately shot or poisoned. In areas where fertile land attracted a denser pattern of European settlement, most of the Aboriginal population perished. Today there are no speakers left of the languages of Tasmania, Victoria and most of New South Wales. The only flourishing languages are to be found in the centre of the continent and along the north coast.

Up until the 1960s government policy was for Aboriginal people to be assimilated, and the white community had a negative attitude towards Aborigines, which induced feelings of shame in Aboriginal people and attempts by part-Aborigines to hide their Aboriginal ancestry. Since then things have changed. Nowadays Aboriginal people are proud of their ancestry, and those who are of part-Aboriginal and part-European descent – the majority in the southeast – identify strongly as Aboriginal and reject the notion of 'part-Aborigine'.

Language classifications

Most of the languages of the Australian mainland share a number of roots such as **nga** for 'I', **bu-** for 'hit' and **ma-** for 'do', and look as if they are related. However, some of the shared forms may be the result of borrowing from one language to another. It is interesting to note that when the first people settled in Australia, the continent included New Guinea and Tasmania, but there are few if any resemblances between the languages of the present-day mainland and those of Tasmania, New Guinea or anywhere else.

FOR MORE INFORMATION...

The indigenous languages of Australia are a huge and complex subject. To learn more, visit www.ourlanguages. net.au.

The mainland languages have been classified into a score or so 'families' on the basis of shared vocabulary. One family, Pama-Nyungan, covers all of the mainland except the Top End of the Northern Territory and the Kimberleys of Western Australia. The word **Pama-Nyungan** was made from **pama** (man) in some of the Cape York languages and **nyunga** (man) in the Perth area.

Another way of classifying the languages is to distinguish between those that use suffixing and those that use prefixing. In the suffixing languages all affixes come at the end of the word, as in English with 'book*s*' and 'slow*ly*'. The prefixing languages have suffixes, but they also have pronoun prefixes on the verb (see the Structure section on p156 for more). The Pama-Nyungan languages are almost all in the suffixing class and almost all the other families of the Top End and the Kimberleys are in the prefixing class.

··

Sounds

In Europe, languages such as French, Italian, German and Polish use very different sounds and thus sound very different from one another. Most Aboriginal languages, however, use much the same set of sounds, so they sound very similar.

Vowels

Many Australian languages have only three distinct vowels, namely *i* as in 'Mimi', *a* as in 'father' and *u*, which can sound like the vowel in 'Lou' or sometimes like the vowel in 'law'. In some languages there are long versions of these vowels as well – basically the same but held longer. The long sounds are written *aa*, *ii* and *uu*.

Consonants

All Australian indigenous languages use the *ng* sound as in 'si**ng**', but it is common for this sound to appear at the beginning of a word, and early recorders often failed to hear it altogether. Initial *ng* occurs in the word for 'I' in a number of languages – Kalkadoon **ngai**, for example. Certain sounds found in English don't occur, such as *s, z, sh, f, v* and *h*.

Another notable feature of Aboriginal languages is that there's normally no distinction between *p* and *b*, *t* and *d*, and *k* and *g*. This is part of the reason that the names of some groups and their languages are spelled in different ways. The Warlpiri people of the Northern Territory, for example, used to be referred to as Walbiri. This can be a problem when it comes to using reference books, particularly where the first sound is the one that can be spelled differently. The name of the original inhabitants of the Adelaide area, for instance, has been spelled both 'Gaurna' and 'Kaurna' (the latter is the community's choice).

There are usually two *r* sounds in Australian languages. One is like the *r* sound in English. It occurs in **mara**, a widespread word for 'hand'. The other is like the *r* sound of Scottish English and is made by flipping the tongue up towards the roof of the mouth or sometimes trilling it. This *r* sound is usually written *rr*. Australian languages also have 'r-coloured' sounds, pronounced in a similar way to how a typical American would say the *r* in the middle of words like 'mourner', 'warder' and 'surly'. The sound occurs, for example, as *rn* in **murnong** (the yam daisy of Victoria) and *rd* (or *rt*) as in **nardoo** (a kind of fern and the flour made from the spores of this fern) – this word is actually **ngardu** and comes from the languages of western New South Wales and neighbouring states. There is also an r-coloured *l* as in **warli**, the Kaurna word for 'hut', which has come into English as 'wurley'.

Some Australian languages have dental sounds (sounds made when the tongue is touching the teeth), written *th* (or *dh*), *nh* and *lh*. Sometimes an underline is used to indicate these sounds (underline is also used in some areas for the r-coloured sounds mentioned above). The Aboriginal *th* sounds a little like *th* in English 'this'. Dental *n* and dental *l* are so similar to ordinary *n* and *l* in English that they can be distinguished only with practice.

Another distinctive feature of Aboriginal languages is a set of 'y-coloured' sounds made by holding the tip of the tongue down behind the lower teeth while pronouncing sounds such as *n, l* and *t*. These sounds are often written with a *y*, as in *ny, ly* and *ty* (also written *tj*). The *ny* occurs in **bunya**, the Yagara name of a tall pine-like tree found in southeastern Queensland. This sound may also occur at the beginning of a word, as in Nyungar, the name of the language and people of southwestern Western Australia. The *ly* sound occurs in Alyawarra, the name of an Arandic language spoken in the southeastern part of the Northern Territory. The *ty* (or *dy*) sound is rather like the *ch* sound or the *j* sound in English. It occurs in **dyarra**, the name of a type of eucalypt from Western Australia. The word has been borrowed from the Nyungar language into English as 'jarrah'.

Word stress

In most Australian languages the main stress falls on the first syllable of a word. In long words there tend to be weak stresses on alternate syllables, as in the Kalkadoon word for boomerang, 'y*á*lkap*à*ri' (stress on the two italicised letters).

Writing

Aboriginal people did not have a system of writing before Europeans arrived. The first Europeans to write down Aboriginal words used English spelling conventions, but English has no consistent way of representing vowel sounds. The letter *u*, for example, represents one sound in 'but' and another in 'put'. In the 20th century it became popular to use the International Phonetic Alphabet (IPA) in which the vowel letters *a, e, i, o* and *u* had the values they have in the words 'Mama', 'Ray', 'Mimi', 'Lolo' and 'Lulu' respectively, and where the letter *j* indicates a *y* sound as in the German *ja*, 'yes'.

Recently there has been a swing away from using IPA, though ŋ (upper case Ŋ) for the *ng* sound has been kept in a few language names such as Yolŋu (the group of languages belonging to northeast Arnhem Land). However, it's not always clear which convention is being used, so pronunciation can be tricky, particularly with a name containing *j* or *u*. There is a language in the north of Western Australia that was previously spelled 'Djaru', but is now 'Jaru', and the *j* is pronounced as in 'jam'. By contrast, in the Top End language Kuniwinjku, the *j* is pronounced *y*, with the *nj* representing the sound found at the end of French words such as *ligne* or *Boulogne*. Similarly, the language of the Yorke Peninsula in South Australia used to be spelled 'Narangga', but the community have adopted the spelling 'Narungga', where the *u* is to be pronounced as in 'but'. The same has happened with Bundjalung, previously 'Bandjalang', a language of the NSW–Queensland border.

Vocabulary

In the past people believed, mistakenly, that Aboriginal languages had only a few words. In fact, like any language, they have thousands. Many of these words don't correspond directly to English words – they express concepts particular to Aboriginal culture.

A striking feature of Aboriginal vocabulary is that the words found in one language are usually quite different from those found in neighbouring languages and elsewhere. This means that if you learn one Aboriginal language, you don't have much of a headstart for learning a second one. However, there are a few words that are widespread. This core of words includes the following:

bina	ear	**bula**	two
mara	hand	**mili**	eye
nyina	sit; remain	**tjalayn**	tongue
tjarra	thigh	**tjina**	foot

Typical Aboriginal words have more than one syllable. They usually begin with a consonant and end with a vowel, and they don't normally contain awkward sequences of consonants that are hard to pronounce. The Arandic languages of central Australia are an exception, however – a number of Arandic artists with tongue-twisting names are represented in Australian art galleries. The following words are fairly representative of a typical Australian language:

barramundi	type of fish, especially *Lates calcarifer* (central Queensland coast)
boobialla	shrubs of the *Myoporum* genus (southeastern Tasmania)
corroboree	ceremony with singing and dancing (Dharuk, Sydney area)
wallaby	kangaroo-like animal (Dharuk, Sydney area)

Structure

Aboriginal languages characteristically use different endings (case suffixes) on nouns and adjectives to mark relations between words in a sentence. In the Kalkadoon language of the Mount Isa area, for instance, a suffix is used to mark the entity responsible for an action. In the following example the ending **-yu** is attached to the word **martu** (mother):

> **Martu-yu ngulurrmai thuku.**
> Mother grabs the dog.

To indicate that the dog grabbed mother, you would put the suffix **-yu** on **thuku** (dog). Because the suffix picks out the actor (ie who's doing the grabbing), the word order can be varied to show different degrees of emphasis. You could have the following order, for instance, which emphasises that it's the dog that's being grabbed:

> **Thuku ngulurrmai martu-yu.**
> Mother grabs the dog.

Here are two more endings: **-piangu** meaning 'from' and **-kunha** meaning 'to':

> **Kanimaintjirr ingka Darwin-piangu Melbourne-kunha.**
> The policeman goes from Darwin to Melbourne.

The word **kanimaintjirr** means 'policeman'. Literally it's 'the one who ties up' – **kanimai** is 'tie up' and **-ntjirr** is a suffix like the *-er* in English words such as 'driver'. It's an interesting example of how the Kalkadoon people made up a word for the new concept of policeman.

The majority of Australian languages attach pronouns to the verb. In a suffixing language like Kalkadoon these are attached to the end of the verb. For example, 'They sent me to town' would be **Town-kunha ngkai-ngi-na** where **ngkai** is 'sent', **-ngi** is 'me' and **-na** is 'they'. In a prefixing language, these pronouns would be attached at the front of the verb. In Kunwinjku, for example, 'I see them' is **Nga-ben-na** where the prefix **nga** is 'I', **ben** is 'them' and **na** is the verb 'to see'. (For those who speak French, it's rather like *Je les vois* – the unstressed pronouns precede the verb.)

Across the north of the continent many of the prefixing languages tend to have very complex verbs that seem more like sentences than single words. In Tiwi, the language of Bathurst and Melville Islands, for instance, the English sentence 'He sent them a message' can be expressed as a single word **yu-wuni-marri-wa-yangirri**, literally 'he-them-with-words-sent'.

New languages

As in other parts of the world where European colonisation and accompanying social disruption have taken place, creole languages have arisen in northern Australia. 'Broken' is a creole spoken in the Torres Strait, and 'Kriol' is a creole spoken by many Aboriginal people across the north of Australia.

The sound system of both Broken and Kriol tends to reflect the traditional sounds of Aboriginal languages. The vocabulary is largely of English origin, mixed with some words from the traditional languages, but the meanings of many of the English words have been changed to refer to traditional concepts and distinctions. For example, in English the word 'we' refers to the speaker and one or more other persons. Aboriginal languages usually have a number of words for 'we', distinguishing between 'we' meaning two people and 'we' meaning more than two, and differing if the addressee (you) is included. These distinctions are carried over into the creoles. In the Kriol of Roper River, for instance, various words have been adapted from English to form the pronouns – **yunmi** means 'we' in the sense of 'you and me', **mintupala** means 'we two (not including you)' and there are a number of words for 'we' covering more than two people. These include **wi**, **melapat** and **mipala**.

Although these new languages have developed, tragically more than half of the original 250 or so Aboriginal languages have lost their last full speakers, some quite recently. However, Aboriginal people all over Australia are showing great interest in preserving what they can of their languages and in trying to restore them from materials recorded during past generations. In many parts of Australia Aboriginal children are being taught the language that belongs to their particular area at school.

Talking with Aboriginal people

Some Aboriginal people in central and northern Australia speak standard Australian English. Others, especially those who speak another language as their first language, may use a different kind of English, often known as Aboriginal English (see the box on p175).

Questions

Asking direct questions (especially 'why' questions such as 'Why aren't you coming?') is considered rude by many Aboriginal people. As a rule, Aboriginal people do not interrogate one other as English speakers tend to do, but rely on each other to be reasonably cooperative in communicating information. It's better to make suggestions or statements or to talk around the issue than to ask direct questions.

Don't embarrass people by asking questions about anything that could be considered private, or expect that someone has time to stop and answer all of your questions. Many Aboriginal people are tired of being harassed by non-Aboriginal people on a search for spiritual or cultural knowledge, but may be too polite to say so.

Greetings

Most Australian languages don't have greetings like 'hello', although Aboriginal people are now accustomed to English speakers using greetings, and some languages have adopted greetings based on the English form. These are used mainly to greet non-Aboriginal people, especially those who have begun to learn the language. Speakers of Aboriginal languages don't use these terms when talking to each other – instead, they often refer to or address others using a relationship term such as 'mother's brother' or a 'skin' name (ie the name of the section of the language group they belong to – see p164).

Please & thank you

Likewise, many Australian languages don't have words for 'please' or 'thank you'. These days, more and more people use the English 'thank you', but thanks is otherwise expressed in actions rather than words. If someone does something for you, you show your thanks by doing something for that person or a relative at a later date. Similarly, if someone gives you something, it's appropriate to give them or one of their relatives something in return at another time – whether it's money, material goods, knowledge or even friendship. If you want to learn something, give something in return.

Names & conversation

It's generally not polite to ask people their name, as many English speakers do, to start a conversation. Among adults, first names are used much less than in non-Aboriginal society. If you really want to know a person's name, ask someone else nearby. A better way of starting a conversation, though, is to refer to a recent local event, or perhaps to admire a child who's accompanying the person you're speaking to. The best way is to tell them where you're from, and ask them where they're from. Aboriginal people, both men and women, always take each other's hand in greeting, with a gentle grip. They will usually expect you to introduce yourself first.

It also isn't polite to talk to a mother-to-be or a father-to-be about the child they're going to have. Aboriginal women may talk among themselves about pregnancy, but questions or interest from a stranger about this topic are likely to embarrass people into an awkward silence.

It's both offensive and upsetting for many Aboriginal people in central and northern Australia to hear the name of a close relative or friend who has recently passed away. The deceased should not be referred to directly – instead, describe a close relative as having lost a son, daughter etc. If someone has the same name, or a name that sounds the same as that of a person who's just passed away, then they may be given a new name, or they may be referred to in English as 'no name', an expression which has equivalents in most Australian languages: **kwementyaye** (Arrernte), **kumanjayi** (Warlpiri) or **kunmanara** (Pitjantjatjara). It's also offensive to show photographs of a person who's recently passed away.

Body & sign language

Many Aboriginal people use hand signs and gestures during both everyday conversation and ceremonies. These signs are not limited to the deaf community, but are used and understood by all speakers. As you walk around towns like Alice Springs or Darwin, you may be aware of people using handsigns to communicate with each other across long distances, like across a river or a busy road, or in other situations where talking or shouting is not practical.

Be aware that Aboriginal people don't use eye contact as much as non-Aboriginal people. There are times, in fact, when eye contact is extremely inappropriate – for example, in certain kin relationships or between men and women who don't know each other.

Kinship systems & politeness

The most important organising principle of Aboriginal society is the kinship system – every member of the community is part of a complex web of kin relations. The kinship system not only means that particular relationships entail certain rights and obligations, but also provides a safety net for Aboriginal people when they are in trouble. Even far from home, the web of connections means that a person will be able to find a 'brother' or 'sister', a friend who will look after them. Aboriginal people travel a lot, and in some states such as Western Australia can expect nearly always to be close to 'family'.

The kinship system determines various patterns of social responsibility, many of which require special forms and styles of speaking. Thus there are rules of politeness and avoidance – traditionally, people would avoid their in-laws or use a special vocabulary when speaking in their presence. Children defer to members of their parents' generation, but interaction between members of the same generation, or between grandparents and grandchildren, is more relaxed and often involves a great deal of joking, teasing and innuendo.

Visitors can show consideration for these rules of politeness by treating older people with respect and reserve and by understanding that, in turn, younger people may treat them with reserve out of simple courtesy, not out of lack of friendliness.

Restrictions

As in most cultures, some knowledge is restricted and cannot be discussed freely. Certain rituals and particular sites, songs, dances and language styles may be restricted. Some objects, decorations or graphic designs may also be restricted and cannot be seen by uninitiated men and women.

All Aboriginal sites are protected under law, whether these are rock paintings or carvings, or scatterings of stone tools in a creek bed. It is an offence to disturb or remove artefacts found in the bush. While not all sites are specifically 'sacred sites', the land itself is sacred in the sense that Aboriginal spirituality embraces the land and everything above and below it. For Aboriginal people, the land is the source of their culture – the stories come from the land.

CENTRAL AUSTRALIA

The languages in central Australia – or the Centre, as it's often called – are among the strongest surviving Aboriginal languages in the country, as their speakers have had a relatively short history of contact with non-Aboriginal people. Despite this, the effects of non-Aboriginal settlement since it began in the 1870s have been dramatic. Before this time, it's thought that there were at least 38 main languages and dialects in the area. The establishment of pastoral properties, the Overland Telegraph Line, missions, reserves and later towns such as Alice Springs has meant that many language groups have moved, or have been moved, from their traditional country. Of the original 38 main languages and dialects, about seven are now considered endangered, and four are considered extinct or nearly extinct.

Language groups

The main surviving language groups in central Australia are the Arandic languages and dialects, dialects of the Western Desert language, dialects of Warlpiri, and Warumungu. These all belong to the Pama-Nyungan family (see p152). The arid lands of central Australia can only support a limited number of people, and as a result, single language groups are spread over vast areas of land. The Western Desert language, for example, is one of the most widely spread indigenous languages in the world, extending from central Australia nearly to the Great Australian Bight and the Indian Ocean. Although languages in the Centre share a few common characteristics, they are for the most part very different from each other. Many people in this region are bilingual or multilingual, speaking one or more Aboriginal languages or dialects and English.

The names of languages and dialects used in central Australia are quite widely known. Often, they describe where the people who speak that language come from, or describe a feature of their language which distinguishes it from another language nearby, for example:

Ikngerre-ipenhe Arrernte 'eastern Arrernte'

Pitjantjatjara 'having the word **pitja**' (come)

Family relationships

Aboriginal people in central Australia think of themselves as related to all the people in their own language group, and often to people in other language groups as well. To regulate social behaviour, law and ceremony, and relationship to land, Aboriginal societies are typically divided into two or three sets of 'moieties' (a moiety is essentially a division of the society into two opposed and balanced halves). In many parts of Australia, the kinship and moiety groupings have been summarised in a neat and efficient way through what are commonly known as 'skin' groups or subsections.

The most common pattern is for there to be eight skin groups, often further divided into male and female groups. A person is born into one of these skin groups and acquires the name of the skin group as well as a personal name. Various relatives are classed together in each skin group, and a person's position within this system determines their relationship and social and ceremonial obligations to all others in the language group.

Arrernte languages

The language name spelt 'Arrernte' in its own spelling system is perhaps better known outside central Australia as 'Aranda' or 'Arunta'. This language is part of a group of closely related languages and dialects known to linguists as the Arandic group (see map, p166). The major language in this group has a number of dialects, including Central, Eastern, Western and Southern Arrernte, Eastern and Western Anmatyerr, and Eastern and Western Alyawarr. There are two smaller languages in the group, not so closely related: Kaytetye to the north and Lower Arrernte, which is no longer spoken, to the south. The territory of the group comprises very roughly the southeastern quarter of the Northern Territory (of which a fairly big chunk, the Simpson Desert, is uninhabitable), and at one time also extended into South Australia north of Oodnadatta. Alice Springs is in Central Arrernte country. There are about 4500 speakers of languages of the group.

Sounds

The Arandic languages are believed to have had sound systems very much like their neighbouring languages, such as Warlpiri and Pitjantjatjara, at some time in the distant past, but they've changed drastically over the centuries. As an example, the word **wama** (snake) has become **apmwe**, **apme** and **mwang** in various dialects.

The most common vowel in Arandic languages is written *e*, but its pronunciation depends very much on what sounds come immediately before and after it. Other vowels are *a* (similar to the *a* in 'father'), in some dialects; *i* (sounds like the vowels in 'air' or 'see', depending on what the next consonant is); and *u* (pronounced like the *u* in 'put' when it begins a word, or like the *o* in 'more' when it comes after the first consonant).

The consonant system is quite complicated, with a number of sounds that exist in almost no other Australian language.

Arandic language group

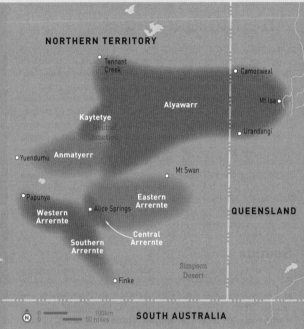

NORTHERN TERRITORY

Tennant
Creek

Camooweal

Mt Isa

Alyawarr

Kaytetye

Barrow
Junction

Urandangi

Yuendumu

Anmatyerr

Mt Swan

Papunya

Eastern
Arrernte

QUEENSLAND

Alice Springs

Western
Arrernte

Central
Arrernte

Southern
Arrernte

Simpson
Desert

Finke

N 0   100km
   0   50 miles

SOUTH AUSTRALIA

Based upon the IAD Language Centre map
  Current Distribution of Central Australian Languages

One unfortunate result, from the point of view of writing, is that some sounds need to be written with two letters (such as *ly, nh, pm, rr, tn*) and some even need three letters (*kng, rtn, tnh, tny*).

Word stress and structure

Stress in Arandic languages is mostly on the vowel that follows the first consonant in a word, although in some dialects short words, such as **artwe** (man) and **iltye** (hand), are stressed on the initial vowel.

The Arandic languages belong to the suffixing category described on page 152.

Vocabulary

Some words that you may come across include:

aherre	red plains kangaroo
akatyerre	desert raisin
altyerre	Dreaming, the Law
alye	boomerang
arelhe	Aboriginal person
arlewatyerre	sand goanna
atneme	woman's digging stick
atyunpe	perentie (large lizard)
inernte	bean tree
irrtyarte	spear
kere	meat or animal used for food
kwatye	water
lhentere	non-Aboriginal person

INDIGENOUS LANGUAGES

merne	food, especially vegetable foods and bread
ngkwarle	sweet things
ntyarlke	elephant grub
pmerlpe	quandong (edible fruit)
rapite	rabbit
tyape	edible grubs
tyerrtye	Aboriginal person
untyeye	corkwood
urtne	coolamon (a shallow wooden dish)
utyerrke	bush fig
warlpele	non-Aboriginal person
yeperenye	caterpillar that lives on the tar vine
yerrampe	honey ant

Place names

The Arrernte name for the Alice Springs area is **Mparntwe**, while Heavitree Gap is **Ntaripe**. The MacDonnell Ranges as a whole are called **Tyurretye** (sometimes spelt **Choritja**). Prominent central Australian mountains include **Rwetyepme** (Mt Sonder), **Urlatherrke** (Mt Zeil) and **Alhekulyele** (Mt Gillen).

Other well-known scenic spots in Arrernte country, in the Eastern MacDonnell Ranges, include:

Anthwerrke	Emily Gap
Ilwentye	Ndhala Gorge
Inteyarrkwe	Ross River
Kepalye	Jessie Gap

And in the Western MacDonnell Ranges:

Angkele	Standley Chasm
Kwartetweme	Ormiston Gorge
Twipethe	Ellery Creek Big Hole
Urrengetyirrpe	Simpsons Gap
Yaperlpe	Glen Helen Gorge

Arrernte place names fall into two groups. One type is when the name describes the place; for example, the Finke River is **Lherepirnte** (anglicised as Larapinta). This is composed of **lhere** (river) and **pirnte** (salt), although there's some doubt about this, as **pirnte** means 'spring (of water)' in some dialects. Likewise, the name of the town Finke is **Aperturl** (usually spelt 'Aputula'), which translates as 'hill-forehead' and refers to a nearby hill.

The second type of name is taken from the Dreaming (Aboriginal creation history) of the area. For example, an area in Alice Springs is called **Ntyarlkarletyaneme** (the place where the elephant grub crosses over). **Ntyarlke** (the elephant grub) is one of the ancestral caterpillar beings which created much of the landscape around Alice Springs, as well as being a kind of caterpillar still found in the area. Some hills in the area covered by the name are parts of the body of these ancestral beings. Further east, in the MacDonnell Ranges, the name for Emily Gap, **Anthwerrke**, means 'small intestine' and refers to the guts of the caterpillar.

··

Western Desert language

The Western Desert language spreads over a vast area of desert country (see the map on the following page). Dialects of Western Desert include Pitjantjatjara, Yankunytjatjara, Ngaanyatjarra, Ngaatjatjarra, Pintupi, Papunya Luritja, Luritja, Matutjara, Kukatja, Antikirinya, Mantjiltjara and Kartutjara.

INDIGENOUS LANGUAGES

Western Desert language group

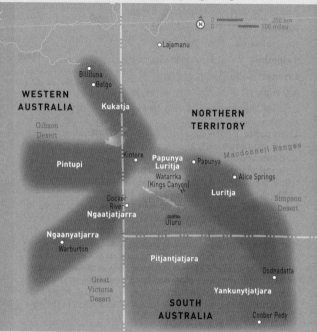

WESTERN AUSTRALIA

Gibson Desert

Great Victoria Desert

Billiluna
Balgo
Kukatja

Pintupi

Kintore

Docker River

Ngaatjatjarra

Ngaanyatjarra
Warburton

Pitjantjatjara

NORTHERN TERRITORY

Lajamanu

Macdonnell Ranges

Papunya Luritja
Papunya

Watarrka (Kings Canyon)

Alice Springs

Luritja

Simpson Desert

Uluru

SOUTH AUSTRALIA

Yankunytjatjara

Oodnadatta

Coober Pedy

0 — 200 km
0 — 100 miles

Based upon the IAD Language Centre map
Current Distribution of Central Australian Languages

In all, it's estimated that there are between 4000 and 5000 speakers of Western Desert dialects, with Pitjantjatjara being one of the better known varieties. Most of the Pitjantjatjara and Yankunytjatjara people live on the Anangu Pitjantjatjara freehold lands in the northwest of South Australia, or just over the borders in Western Australia and the Northern Territory.

Vocabulary

Some words that you may come across are:

anangu	Aboriginal person
anumara	edible caterpillar
ili	bush fig
ininti	bean tree
kali	boomerang
kampurarpa	desert raisin
kapi	water
katji/kulata	spear
kuka	meat or animal used for food
kurku	honeydew on mulga (an acacia shrub)
mai	food, especially vegetable foods and bread
maku	edible grubs, especially witchetty grubs (a grub that lives in the roots of the witchetty bush)
malu	red plains kangaroo
ngintaka	perentie (large lizard)
piranpa	non-Aboriginal person
piti	coolamon (shallow wooden bowl used to carry water)
rapita	rabbit

tinka	sand goanna
tjala	honey ant
tjukurpa	Dreaming, the Law
walypala	non-Aboriginal person
wama	sweet things (nowadays also used to refer to alcohol)
wana	women's digging stick
wayanu	quandong (edible fruit)
witjinti	corkwood

Place names

Both of Uluru and Kata Tjuta are on the border between Pitjantjatjara and Yankunytjatjara country. The name 'Uluru' is thought by some people to be derived from **ulerenye**, an Arrernte word for 'stranger'. **Kata Tjuta** translates into English as 'heads' or 'many heads'.

Pitjantjatjara and Yankunytjatjara people call tourists **minga tjuta** (ants). If you stand at the base of Uluru, and watch people climbing, you'll understand why. The traditional owners of Uluru would prefer that you didn't climb the rock.

....

Warlpiri

Languages & dialects

Warlpiri is part of the Ngarrkic language group (see the map opposite). There are thought to be at least 3000 Warlpiri speakers, most of whom speak Warlpiri as their first language. They live in a number of quite large communities around the edge of traditional Warlpiri country: Yurntumu (Yuendumu), Lajamanu (which used to be called Hooker Creek, and is actually on Kurindji country), Wirliyajarrayi (Willowra) and Nyirrpi (which

Ngarrkic language group

Language locations approximate only.

Based upon the IAD Language Centre map
 Current Distribution of Central Australian Languages

is strictly speaking a Pintupi community). But many Warlpiri spend at least part of the year in the numerous out-stations (small communities) in Warlpiri country, the heart of which is the Tanami Desert (named by Europeans after Janami rock-hole, near the junction of the Tanami road and the Lajamanu road). There are also substantial Warlpiri populations in other communities around traditional Warlpiri country, especially on Kaytetye country in Alekarenge (a Kaytetye name referring to Dog Dreaming, also written 'Ali Curung' and which used to be called Warrabri), and in towns such as Alice Springs on Arrernte country, Tennant Creek on Warumungu country and Katherine on Jawoyn country.

Warlpiri is still a very vigorous language, and though it's being lost by Warlpiri children in some communities that lie outside the traditional country (usually to Aboriginal English or an Aboriginal creole), it's nonetheless spreading well outside its traditional country, and is also spoken by 1000 or more people as a second language over a very large area extending as far north as Darwin, west to Fitzroy Crossing in Western Australia, east to Tennant Creek and other Barkly Tableland communities, and south to Alice Springs and the northern Western Desert communities.

There are five major dialects of Warlpiri: Warrmarla or Ngardilypa to the west, Warnayaka to the north, Ngaliya to the south, Yarlpiri or Warlpiri in the Lander River area in the heart of Warlpiri country, and Wakirti Warlpiri in the Hansen River area to the east. The main differences are in vocabulary and pronunciation, reflecting the influences of neighbouring languages, but they are mutually comprehensible. Though the Warlpiri will sometimes emphasise the dialect differences, they generally consider themselves to be one people with one language, Warlpiri.

Warlpiri has a spelling system which has been in use since 1974, mainly in the context of bilingual education programs in the schools of the main Warlpiri communities. Nowadays, most young to middle-aged Warlpiri can read and write their language.

ABORIGINAL ENGLISH

Aboriginal people often speak a distinctive form of English. In southeastern Australia this differs from mainstream English in that there are old-fashioned English words like **plant** (to hide) and **gammon** (to pretend or to deceive), plus some Aboriginal words such as **binjy** (stomach) and **bogey** (to bathe). These are words from the Sydney area that have been widely disseminated. It's also common to find words such as **kuna** (faeces) and **marra** (hand) which are widespread in Aboriginal languages, plus some words from local languages.

In the north of Australia, Aboriginal English exhibits the same features as in the south plus various degrees of similarity to Kriol (see p158). Aboriginal people are likely to use **he** and **fella** for females as well as males, for instance, or use **mother** for their mother's sister as well as their real mother. Past tense is rendered by **bin**, and **longa** or **alonga** substitutes for a variety of English prepositions, so we find **That one bin fightin' alonga nother fella** for 'That one was fighting with another person'. That's clear enough, but the use of **meself** as a general reflexive pronoun is confusing. **Them blackfellas bin fightin meself** sounds as if it means 'Those Aborigines were fighting me', but in fact it means 'Those Aborigines were fighting one another'.

Aboriginal English often includes English words used with ranges of meaning that match those of words from Aboriginal languages. **Shame**, for instance, covers modesty as well as shame, and the types of breach of good conduct that are grounds for shame are wider than in European culture. Another example is the expression **no more**, which can correspond to 'no more' in English or can simply mean 'no' or 'not'.

Vocabulary

Some words that you may come across:

jukurrpa	Dreaming, the Law
jurlarda	bush honey
kardiya	non-Aboriginal person
karli	boomerang
kuyu	meat or animal used for food
mangarriyi	food, especially vegetable foods and bread
marlu	red plains kangaroo
miyi	food, especially vegetable foods and bread
ngapa	water
ngarlkirdi	witchetty grub
ngayaki	bush tomato
ngurlu	grain; seeds
pama	delicacy (nowadays also used to refer to alcohol)
parraja	coolamon; dish used to separate grains and chaff, and carry babies and food
wardapi	sand goanna
yankirri	emu
yapa	Aboriginal person
yarla	bush potato

TOP END

In the 'Top End', the northern half of the Northern Territory, there are a large number of languages of the prefixing type, though there is also an enclave of Pama-Nyungan languages in northeast Arnhem Land.

....

European influence

The history of the European settlement of the Top End is important to the understanding of the present linguistic situation. In areas where Europeans settled early and in large numbers, such as around the Darwin region and southwards along the Stuart Highway, traditional languages are no longer spoken.

In the drier open savannah country, cattle stations were set up using the labour of Aboriginal people. Aboriginal station 'employees' – their wage and living conditions often amounted to little better than slavery – had to be able to communicate in English. It's difficult to generalise about the effect that cattle

LANGUAGE & CULTURE

Membership in a particular language is of great social and cultural significance, and land, language and people are inextricably bound together in Aboriginal culture. Traditionally, languages belong to tracts of country (often having been put there by Dreamtime creator figures); therefore, Aboriginal people belong to their country and to their languages. Ownership of particular country and its associated language(s) is inherited through either or both parents, depending on the area.

stations had on Top End language groups. Where Aboriginal 'employees' were predominantly from the same language group, as at Wave Hill Station (Gurindji language group) and Humbert River Station (Ngarinyman language group), it was possible for people to continue speaking their traditional language in some situations, such as in the camp or out bush. The seasonal nature of the work – there was little or no work available during the Wet – also meant that Aboriginal 'employees' relied upon their traditional knowledge to survive.

Around the Top End coastline missions were established; their effect on Aboriginal language groups depended a great deal on the individual institution and on the circumstances of the area. In some instances, missionaries forbade the use of traditional languages, whereas in others Europeans working with a mission were expected to learn the traditional languages. At some missions, the so-called dormitory system was enforced, whereby children were housed separately from their parents in dormitories. This was particularly disruptive to the transmission of traditional languages.

Land rights

In recent years, many Aboriginal language groups have been able to claim back (part of) their traditional lands. However, not all Aboriginal groups have been able to regain possession of their land, due to provisions in legislation about the kind of land that can be claimed and who can be recognised as traditional owners.

It was in part the regaining of the ownership of and access to traditional lands that made the homeland centres movement possible. 'Homeland centre' is the term commonly used in the north-east region for what in other areas are called 'out-stations' – small communities in a group's traditional country. The movement began in the 1970s and saw family groups opting to move out of larger communities to their traditional lands to start homeland centres with populations of 15 to 100.

The Top End today

The Top End languages provide examples of all the possible post-colonial fates of indigenous languages – from no speakers at all to full use in all everyday activities.

In areas with large, long-term European settlement like Darwin and Katherine, the traditional languages are no longer spoken. Any traditional languages spoken by Aboriginal people in these places are from other areas. In Darwin, this could be Tiwi from Bathurst or Melville Islands or one of the Yolŋu languages from East Arnhem Land, among many other possibilities. In Katherine, visitors might hear Warlpiri from the desert country in the far southwest of the region.

Traditional Aboriginal languages are still spoken in more isolated areas where contact with non-Aboriginal people has been most recent. Areas where traditional languages are still fully spoken include the Daly River region southwest of Darwin, Bathurst and Melville Islands to the north of Darwin, the Arnhem Land Reserve to the east, Groote Eylandt in the Gulf of Carpentaria and the desert region at the southwestern edge of the Top End.

In many areas with a lot of non-Aboriginal visitors, such as Kakadu National Park, Litchfield or Nitmiluk (Katherine Gorge), only older members of the Aboriginal community know their ancestral languages fluently. Younger people may well understand and use some traditional language but they mostly speak Kriol, a dialect of Aboriginal English or another traditional language.

Language shift

In communities where traditional languages continue to be used, some languages are growing in numbers of speakers while others are declining. This is due to language shifts from one traditional language to another, in part because of changing demographic patterns. Formerly, small numbers of people lived in isolated clan groups and this isolation fostered the maintenance of many distinct language varieties. These days, even in relatively isolated areas, people tend to live for at least some of the year in large regional communities populated by members of different language groups. In such multilingual communities there's a trend for one language to emerge as a lingua franca.

Katherine Region

Aboriginal people nowadays use the terms 'sun-go-down' (or 'sunset') to refer to the people, lands and languages in the western Katherine Region (approximately west of the Stuart Highway), and 'sunrise' to refer to those in the east of the region. This division reflects the perceived differences in the nature of the languages, in the groups they're affiliated with, in traditional culture, in climate and country, and even in art styles. (Abstract 'dot paintings' are typical of the western Katherine Region, whereas figures and lined artwork typify the east side.)

Katherine

The township of Katherine is the administrative centre of the region and it's possible to find members of all the language groups of the Katherine Region there as well as many others from even further afield. Of the three Aboriginal languages traditionally spoken in and around Katherine, Dagoman is no longer spoken and Jawoyn is spoken only by some older people. Wardaman is slightly 'stronger' in that it's been transmitted to some younger people who speak or understand it. The Aboriginal language that visitors to Katherine will definitely hear is Kriol. With the exception of Lajamanu in the far southwest, Aboriginal communities have a variety of Kriol as a first or main language.

Sun-go-down (western region)

The country is drier here than elsewhere in the Top End, as the Victoria River is the only major river system in the entire region. There are four main areas of Aboriginal population, from south to north: Lajamanu; Daguragu and Kalkaringi; Pigeon Hole, Yarralin and Lingara; and communities in the environs of Timber Creek.

Lajamanu is now a Warlpiri-speaking community, because white authorities moved large numbers of Warlpiri people away from their traditional homelands further south and onto lands traditionally owned by Kartangarrurru and Gurindji people. At Lajamanu, children are still acquiring Warlpiri as their first language.

At Kalkaringi (the old government settlement of Wave Hill) and Daguragu (the old strike camp of Wattie Creek), however, Gurindji is still spoken, although the main language of the children and young adults is a variety of Kriol that is influenced by Gurindji. Even so, children and young people mostly have a thorough understanding of Gurindji as well. The Gurindji people are famous for the Wave Hill Strike of 1966, which fought back at the shocking wage and living conditions endured by Aboriginal people working on cattle stations at that time and which eventuated in a fight for land rights.

To the east of Gurindji is Mudburra, which is spoken across the region as far as Elliott. To the west are Nyininy and Malngin, language varieties that are closely related to Gurindji.

Bilinarra country lies to the north of Gurindji around the Pigeon Hole and Yarralin communities. However, Ngarinyman is the main traditional language represented at Yarralin and it's spoken over a large area to the northwest as far as Kununurra and northwards to communities around Timber Creek.

Speakers of four main language groups have settled in communities in and around Timber Creek: Ngarinyman, Ngaliwurru, Nungali and Jaminjung. Traditional country for the Ngaliwurru includes the spectacular Stokes Ranges. Jaminjung

Aboriginal languages of the Katherine Region

Language locations approximate only.

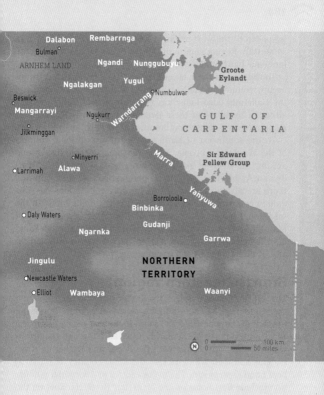

Dalabon Rembarrnga

Bulman

ARNHEM LAND

Ngandi Nunggubuyu

Groote
Eylandt

Ngalakgan Yugul

Beswick

Mangarrayi

Ngukurr Warndarrang Numbulwar

Jilkminggan

GULF OF
CARPENTARIA

Minyerri

Larrimah Alawa

Marra

Sir Edward
Pellew Group

Yanyuwa

Borroloola

Daly Waters Binbinka

Ngarnka Gudanji

Garrwa

NORTHERN
TERRITORY

Jingulu

Newcastle Waters

Elliot Wambaya

Waanyi

0   100 km
0   50 miles

WA   NT   QLD

SA   NSW

VIC

TAS

is spoken to the west as far as Kununurra and to the north in some Daly Region communities. It's believed that the Nungali language has become extinct.

To the west of these languages, two further language groups occupy country in the Northern Territory: the Miriwoong and the Gajirrang (also known as Gajirrabeng and Gajirrawoong), although members of these language groups mostly reside in Kununurra and nearby communities in Western Australia today.

To the southwest of Katherine lies the traditional country of the Wardaman people. Most Wardaman people live in and around the town of Katherine nowadays. However, the Wardaman Association owns and operates Innesvale Station and there are also a number of small family out-stations on Wardaman country. Wardaman was mutually intelligible with the traditional languages spoken near Katherine (Dagoman) and Mataranka (Yangman). However, unlike Dagoman and Yangman, which are no longer spoken, Wardaman is still spoken and/or understood by some younger people today.

Sunrise (eastern region)

The 'sunrise' (eastern) side of the Katherine Region extends from the Stuart Highway across to the 'saltwater country' bordering the Gulf of Carpentaria. From south to north it reaches from the 'dry country' north of the Barkly Tableland, through the 'freshwater country' associated with the Roper and Katherine River systems and their tributaries, to the 'stone country' of the Arnhem Land escarpment. The major centres of Aboriginal population include Borroloola on the McArthur River, Ngukurr on the Roper River, Minyerri (formerly Hodgson Downs), Jilkminggan at the headwaters of the Roper, and the communities of Barunga, Beswick and Bulman on the Central Arnhem Highway.

Borroloola is situated on the traditional country of the Yanyuwa, although members of surrounding language groups such as Garrwa, Gudanyji and Marra all live in and around Borroloola nowadays. An interesting feature of Yanyuwa is that women's speech is structurally different to the variety spoken by men. The differences include a separate system of prefixes used when a woman is talking about a man – she must use the prefix **ny(a)-** on the noun and any adjectives referring to him:

'You disobedient boy!'

woman speaking:	man speaking:
yenda ny-ardu nya-mordo	**yenda ardu mordo**
(lit: you boy deaf)	(lit: you boy deaf)

To the north of Borroloola, on the Roper River, is the community of Ngukurr and several smaller communities and out-stations. The linguistic situation here is highly complex. People affiliated with numerous language groups, including Ngalakgan, Warndarrang (also spelt 'Warndarraŋ'), Yugul, Marra, Ngandi, Alawa, Nunggubuyu, Ritharrŋu and Rembarrnga, now live at Ngukurr. Of these languages, Warndarrang, Yugul, Ngandi and Ngalakgan are believed to be no longer spoken, and Alawa and Marra are spoken fully only by some older people. Rembarrnga and Ritharrŋu probably have relatively greater numbers of speakers in more remote communities.

Minyerri and Jilkminggan, communities further east in the Roper Valley, are on Alawa and Mangarrayi country respectively. The writings of Jeannie Gunn, such as *We of the Never-Never*, were based on her experiences of Elsey Station in Mangarrayi country. Mangarrayi, like Alawa and Marra mentioned above, is only spoken fully by some older people.

The Barunga, Beswick and Bulman communities are located in Central Arnhem Land to the north of the Roper Valley on the Central Arnhem Highway. Barunga and Beswick were formerly part of Bamyili, a government reserve. The traditional owners for this country are Jawoyn. The popular tourist destinations Nitmiluk (Katherine Falls) and Leliny (Edith Falls) are also on Jawoyn country. However, speakers from other language groups – including Mayali, Dalabon and Rembarrnga – form a large proportion of the population at Barunga and Beswick. At Bulman, the major language groups represented are Dalabon and Rembarrnga, which are spoken fully by some older adults – younger adults tend to be able to understand their traditional languages but don't usually speak them fully.

Kriol

Kriol is a new Aboriginal language that has upwards of 20,000 speakers throughout most of the Katherine Region and the neighbouring Kimberley Region in Western Australia. The name 'Kriol' has been applied to it relatively recently and has not yet gained widespread currency among all of its speakers.

As the name suggests, Kriol is a creole language – this means that it's a kind of 'emergency language' which has a specific origin. Kriol first arose early in the 20th century when surviving members of many decimated language groups fled to the Roper River Mission to escape the brutal killings being carried out by cattle station companies in the area at that time. Many of the adults who came to the Roper River Mission were multilingual, but they were certainly not multilingual in exactly the same languages. Moreover, their children had not yet developed full competence in as many languages. In this situation, the only form of language available for communication among everybody – including the English-speaking missionaries – was a pidgin that had entered the Northern Territory a few decades previously with the cattle trade and had become fairly widespread. Children at the mission heard more of this pidgin than any other language, not least because the missionaries housed them in dormitories away from their elders. The children acquired the pidgin as their first language and, in doing so, created a full language which was able to meet all their communicative needs.

Due to its origins, Kriol has elements in common with traditional Aboriginal languages, with English and with other creole languages. As 'new' languages, creole languages tend to have fewer of the irregularities that occur in older languages and they also tend to convey most kinds of linguistic meaning with separate words. So whereas English can use the ending *-ed* to indicate past time, Kriol always uses a separate word, **bin**, to indicate an action that happened in the past. For example, **bin luk** means 'looked'.

Vocabulary

Kriol speakers use large numbers of words from their traditional languages, especially in areas of traditional knowledge such as place names, traditional items like boomerangs and coolamons, names for local flora and fauna, and for personal information like Aboriginal personal names, relationship terms and body parts. Kriol speakers who live in different areas draw on different traditional Aboriginal languages for this kind of vocabulary, so Kriol can vary a great deal from place to place.

Structure

In some ways Kriol also resembles traditional Aboriginal languages structurally. For instance, many traditional Aboriginal languages and Kriol don't have a class of separate adjectives.

Nouns

Kriol uses a variety of words preceding nouns to indicate plurals. However, there's a fair amount of leeway in Kriol as to whether plurals are marked or not – sometimes it's already obvious from the context if the reference is plural.

ola	*plural marker*
ola biliken	(the) billycans
ola kenggurru	(the) kangaroos

If Kriol speakers are referring to just two of something (dual number), they have to mark this with **dubala** (sometimes **tubala**).

dubala/tubala	*dual marker*
dubala gel	(the) two girls

Verbs

Kriol indicates past time with the marker **bin** before a verb, as mentioned on p187. For example:

Minbala bin wok gada ola biliken.
The two of us walked with the billycans.

This joins with the form **im** (he/she/it) to make **imin**:

imin laithad la melabat
he said to all of us
(lit: he-was like-that to all-of-us)

Once a story has been established in the past, Kriol doesn't necessarily mark every instance of a verb with **bin**.

Future time (and also necessity) are expressed with the marker **gada** (or **garra**) before a verb. This marker sounds the same as some of the forms of the word **gada** meaning 'with', so it can be a little confusing:

Yumob gada gu gada yumob matha.
You lot *will* go with your mother.
You lot *have to* go with your mother.

Kriol has some interesting tools for indicating 'a lot of' an action or an event. These can be used independently or they can be combined to achieve various nuances. If describing something that would occur regularly or habitually, Kriol uses the marker **oldei** meaning 'usually', 'habitually', 'always', 'would' etc (often shortened to **ala**). Oldei was originally derived from the English expression 'all day', but obviously doesn't have much in common with it now.

Melabat bin oldei gu fishing en hanting.
> We all would go fishing and hunting.
> We all usually went fishing and hunting.

If there's a lot of something happening – for example, when a lot of people are involved, or there's a repeated series of events – Kriol often doubles up the verb:

Mela bin gula-gula gija olawei.
> We were telling off each other all the way.

If something happens for an uninterrupted time span (especially when this is subsequently interrupted or ended), Kriol speakers will often lengthen or stretch out a word as they say it. The pitch of the lengthened word is markedly higher than the surrounding words, so it sounds almost like singing.

Minbala bin oldei wok-w-o-o-o-k.
> The two of us would keep on walking.

Kriol doesn't have any one item that's directly equivalent to the English verb 'to be'. To indicate the meaning 'to be in a place or state', the Kriol verb **jidan** (sometimes also **sidan**), 'stay', 'stop', 'sit', may be used:

jidan kwait
> stay quiet, be quiet

Mela ol jidan la kemp.
> We all stop in the camp.
> We are all in the camp.

However, where the orientation of something is important, such as vertical versus horizontal, or is inherent in its nature (for example, trees 'stand' in Kriol), Kriol always prefers the use of more specific verbs, like **jendap** (stand, be vertical).

To say 'something is something' (ie 'X is Y'), Kriol just places the items together with no intervening element:

Thad trubala.
> That is true.

Kriol remains primarily a spoken language, used for everyday communication in all-Aboriginal contexts. Various bands from the Katherine Region have used Kriol in their songs. However, it's also used as a language of instruction and in initial literacy work in the bilingual school program at Barunga Community, where many Kriol texts for children have been produced. There's also a Kriol Bible translation and a Kriol–English dictionary.

Darwin & the nearby islands

Larrikiya is the language of the traditional owners of Darwin (see the map on p194). Today it's spoken only by a few elderly people. For other languages of the Darwin region, such as Wuna and Limilngan, the situation is the same. You'll certainly hear many different Aboriginal languages spoken on the streets of Darwin, but none of them will be Larrikiya. The languages you'll hear will be indigenous to other areas, spoken by people who are immigrants or visitors to town.

Tiwi continues to be spoken on Bathurst and Melville Islands immediately to the north of Darwin. Traditional Tiwi is a highly complex language, although under the influence of English a simpler variety has arisen with fewer affixes and fewer of those words that correspond to whole sentences in English.

Northern central region

Most of the languages spoken in the interior part of the Top End are related to one another as members of the Kunwinjkuan family. Languages in this family include Warray, Jawoyn, Bininj Kunwok (with dialects including Mayali, Kunwinjku, Kuninjku and Kune), Kunbarlang, Rembarrnga, Dalabon (also called Dangbon and

Ngalkbon), Ngalakgan, Ngandi and Nunggubuyu. Kunwinjkuan languages are spoken around the Arnhem Land escarpment.

Warray is spoken by a few elderly people in the Pine Creek area. Jawoyn is spoken by some older people in Katherine, Pine Creek, Barunga and Beswick, around the southwestern edge of the escarpment. Bininj Kunwok – literally, 'people's language' – is a series of dialects spoken in a chain around the western and northern rim of the escarpment. Mayali is in the west, Kunwinjku in the northwest (Gunbalanya area), Kuninjku in the Liverpool River area and Kune on the eastern rim of the escarpment.

Dalabon (also known as Dangbon and Ngalkbon) and Rembarrnga are traditionally spoken around the eastern edge of the escarpment. Dalabon and Rembarrnga are today spoken on the northern rim of the escarpment at homeland centres such as Korlobidahda, Buluh Karduru and Malnjangarnak, and also at communities situated south of the escarpment such as Bulman, Beswick and Barunga. Both the Ngalakgan and Ngandi languages, once spoken to the southeast towards the Roper River region, are today believed extinct.

Maningrida is an important regional centre and is situated in a transitional area between east and west Arnhem Land. There are significant cultural differences between Arnhem Landers who affiliate with the 'west side' and those who affiliate with the 'east side'. Burarra people affiliate with the east side and the Burarra language has been used in albums recorded by the Maningrida Sunrize Band. A variety of Bininj Kunwok is the language of the inhabitants of Maningrida who are affiliated with the west side.

Structure

Kunwinjkuan languages have complex verbs with pronouns prefixed to the verb and object nouns incorporated into the verb. For example, in Kunwinjku, **Birri-gug-nang** is 'They saw the body' with **birri** 'they', **gug** 'body' and **nang** 'saw'.

Aboriginal languages of north-central Top End

ARAFURA SEA

Cobourg Peninsula
Marrgu
Garrik
Iwaja
Mawng
Van Dieman Gulf
Amurdak
Kunbarlang
Maningrida
Ndjebbana
Nakkara
Burarra
Djinaŋ
Milingimbi
Elcho Is
Dhuwala
Ngaduk
Limilngan
oOenpelli (Gunbalanya)
Kuninjku
Gurrgoni
Ramingining
Djinba
Gaagudju
oJabiru
Kunwinjku
Gunnartpa
Kune
Gun-Djeihmi
Rembarrnga
Ritharrŋu
Mayali
Dalabon
ARNHEM LAND
oBulman
Ngandi
oPine Creek
NORTHERN TERRITORY
Ngalakgan
Nunggubuyu
Numbulwar
Jawoyn
Maranboy oo Barunga
Warndarrang
Dagoman
oKatherine
oBeswick
oRoper
Mataranka
Mangarrayi
Roper Bar
oNgukurr
Maria Is
Yangman
Port Roper
Wardman
Alawa

North-central Top End languages

These languages represent a 'chain' of languages that are spoken contiguously around the Arnhem Land escarpment; they are 'closer' to each other than the other languages shown here.

Language locations approximate only.

Most Kunwinjkuan languages have a system of grammatical gender or noun classes, usually four classes: masculine, feminine, plant and inanimate. Noun classes are usually marked by prefixes and these prefixes can also show up on adjectives and verbs. Here are examples of noun class agreement in Kunbarlang.

barbung na-rleng lots of fish (lit: fish *masculine*-lots)

balbarlak ki-rleng lots of crabs (lit: crab *feminine*-lots)

mardugudj ma-rleng lots of plums (lit: plum *plant*-lots)

kuwalak ku-rleng lots of rocks (lit: rock *inanimate*-lots)

Northern Kunwinjkuan languages (Mayali, Kunwinjku and Kunbarlang) have free word order in the sentence and no case endings (ie no markings on nouns to show what their role is in the sentence). All the work of tracking who's doing what to whom is done using the prefixes on verbs. Southern Kunwinjkuan languages (Warray, Jawoyn, Dalabon, Rembarrnga, Ngalakgan, Ngandi and Nunggubuyu), however, have case endings on nouns as well as prefixes on verbs.

Along the coast and the major river systems of the Top End (the Roper in the east, the Daly in the west) there's great diversity among language groups. Like the Kunwinjkuan languages, the languages in this area use complex systems of prefixes on nouns and verbs – note that Yolŋu languages don't, however.

The Daly region

Languages of the Daly region, southwest of Darwin, belong to several groups. Murrinh-Patha (also spelt 'Murrin-Patha') has become one of the more widely spoken languages in the region (see the map on p194). At Wadeye (Port Keats), one of the major communities in the region, members of eight language groups moved in from their traditional countries to live at the mission. Missionaries encouraged the use of Murrinh-Patha, the

Aboriginal languages of northwest Top End

Cobourg Peninsula
Garrik
Marrgu
Croker Island

Melville Island
Tiwi

Tiwi
Bathurst Island

Clarence Strait

Van Dieman Gulf

Dundas Strait

Beagle Gulf

Ngaduk

TIMOR SEA

Darwin
Palmerston
Larrikiya

Wuna
Limilngan

Jabiru

Batchelor
Kungarakany
Warray

Bark Hut Inn
Umbugarla
Uwinymil

Adelaide River

NORTHERN TERRITORY

Menniefe
Fatjifamani
Emmi Kuwema
Kendjerra-
Math
Malak
Malak

Daly River
Kamu

Pine Creek

Marri-
syevin
Marri-Amu
Mara-
Nunggu

Matngele

Wagiman

Jawoyn

Mati Ke

Wadeye (Port Keats)
Murrinh-
Patha

Marri-
Ngarr
Murrinh-
Kura

Marri-
Dan

Marra-
Maninjeji
Ngan'gi-
Kurunggur
Ngen'gi-
Wumirri

Dagoman
Katherine

Joseph Bonaparte Gulf

Wardaman

Yangman

WESTERN AUSTRALIA

Gajirrang

Miriwoong

Kununurra

Jaminjung

Timber Creek

Nungali

Ngaliwurru

100 km
50 miles

Language locations approximate only.

WA

NT

QLD

SA

NSW

VIC

TAS

language of the traditional owners of the country in which the mission was located. A Murrinh-Patha Bible was produced, and a dictionary and other documentary materials compiled. Subsequently the school introduced a bilingual education program in Murrinh-Patha.

Partly as a result of these initiatives, Murrinh-Patha gradually became the standard language of the whole community. An unintended side effect has been that few young people now speak any traditional language other than Murrinh-Patha fluently and almost no children understand community languages other than Murrinh-Patha. This is perceived as a serious issue by the community, so the school and the local language centre have begun documenting the other community languages.

Structure

Languages in the Daly region have a structure typical of prefixing languages, but they make more use of classifiers (words that describe the 'class' a noun falls into – food or animals, for example) than most others. In many Australian languages a generic classifier is used with a specific noun, so that you would say 'vegetable-food yam' rather than just 'yam'. It is possible to use various classifiers with a particular noun to indicate different properties or aspects. For example, in the Mati Ke (or Mati Ge) language of the Wadeye area, the word **marri** means 'cycad', a palm-like plant. If you put the classifier for 'things' in front of it, the combination just refers to the plant. If you use the 'vegetable-food' marker, the meaning is 'ripe cycad nuts'. If you use the 'animal' classifier, it refers to a cockroach that lives in the dead fronds:

awu marri	bush cockroach that lives in dead cycad fronds ('animal' class)
miyi marri	ripe cycad nuts ('food' class)
nhanjdji marri	cycad plant ('thing' class)

Northeast Arnhem Land

Arnhem Land is a reserve that was created in 1933. The Aboriginal population in this region is distributed between eight main communities (Ramingining, Milingimbi, Gapuwiyak, Galiwin'ku, Yirrkala, Umbakumba, Angurugu and Numbulwar) and numerous homeland centres. Most non-Aborigines in the region are there for work, either in Aboriginal communities (in schools, clinics and so on) or in the mining towns of Nhulunbuy and Alyangula. As a result of the shift towards self-determination in the 1970s, an increasing number of Aboriginal people hold positions previously dominated by non-Aborigines.

The languages of the northeast corner of Arnhem Land are of the Pama-Nyungan family. They have become commonly known outside the region as the Yolŋu languages. (The *o* in Yolŋu is pronounced like a long version of the *u* in 'put'.) In this area, there are some 50 clans and each clan claims to speak a distinct language variety. The relationship of these languages to each other is complex – imagine a patchwork quilt of lands belonging to different clans woven together by spiritual, ceremonial and linguistic threads made by the Ancestral Beings. Land, clan, song, ceremony and languages are all linked together.

One local way of grouping different clan language varieties is to divide languages according to the word they use for 'this' or 'here'. Clans such as Gälpu (Gaalpu), Rirratjiŋu (Rirratjingu), Golumala (Guulumala) and Wangurri use **dhaŋu** and clans such as Djambarrpuyŋu, Liyagawumirr and Djapu use **dhuwal**. Within the Yolŋu languages (shown on the map opposite) there are five or six of these larger groupings.

The Yolŋu languages in this northeast corner are surrounded by the non-Pama-Nyungan type. From the northwest these are Burarra, Rembarrnga, Ngandi, Nunggubuyu on the mainland and Anindilyakwa, the language of Groote Eylandt. To this day, groups within a geographical area intermarry and children are raised with different languages spoken around the hearth. In

Aboriginal languages of northeast Arnhem Land

WESSEL
ISLANDS
Marchinbar Is

ARAFURA SEA

Drysdale Is

Guluwuru Is

Mooroongga Is Yan-nhaŋu
Yabooma Is
Milingimbi
Burarra Djinaŋ Howard Is
Ramingining Banyan Is

Elcho Is
Galiwinku
Inglis Is
Nhaŋu
Dhaŋu
Dhuwal
Dhuwala
Dhuwal
Arnhem Bay
Dhaŋu
Dhuwala
Dhaŋu
Dhuwal
Dhuwala
Yirrkala
Dhuwal
Nhulunbuy

Djinaŋ

Gapuwiyak Dhuwala

Djinba

Ritharrŋu

Rembarrnga

Dha'yi Dhaŋu
Dhuwala
Dhuwal
Dhuwala
Garrthalala

ARNHEM LAND

NORTHERN
TERRITORY

Ritharrŋu
Dha'yi

Ritharrŋu

Dhuwala

Bulman

Ngandi

Isle
Woodah

Nunggubuyu

Ngandi

GULF
OF
CARPENTARIA

Anindilyakwa
Bickerton
Is
Angurugu
Milyakburra
Alyangula
GROOTE
EYLANDT
Umbakumba

Anindilyakwa

Numbulwar

0 ___ 50 km
0 ___ 25 miles

- **Northeast Arnhem Land languages**
- **Yolŋu languages**

Language locations approximate only.

Based on a map supplied by the Northern
Territory Department of Education.

WA NT QLD
SA NSW
VIC
TAS

all communities, the population is still multilingual and almost all languages in the region still have speakers. However, some have very few speakers and the population of speakers of several varieties is ageing.

The most widely spoken Yolŋu varieties are, from west to east: Djinaŋ, spoken around Ramingining; a Dhuwal variety usually referred to as Djambarrpuyŋu (but somewhat different to the traditional Djambarrpuyŋu) spoken from Milingimbi to Gapuwiyak; and Dhuwaya, a koine (a new Yolŋu language) that has evolved around Yirrkala. At Numbulwar, Kriol is the first language of most young people but there's a major effort being undertaken in the community to maintain other languages, particularly Nunggubuyu. Anindilyakwa is still the first language of indigenous people on Groote Eylandt.

WESTERN AUSTRALIA

There are two broad types of language in Western Australia. Those spoken in the Kimberley, roughly north of the Fitzroy River, are of the prefixing type, like the languages of the Top End of the Northern Territory. The remainder are purely suffixing (see page 152 for details on suffixing and prefixing).

Most Aboriginal people over the age of 30 in the Kimberley, Pilbara and Western Desert regions speak one or more traditional languages. Throughout most of the state, Aboriginal people, except possibly the elderly, also speak English. There's an array of varieties of Aboriginal English, ranging from close to standard Australian English, through to varieties very close to Kriol (see p158).

European influence

The European settlement of Western Australia began with the establishment of the Swan River colony (Perth) in 1829 and spread to other parts of the state over the next 50 years, with agriculture and the pastoral industry, pearl fishing on the Pilbara and Kimberley coasts, and gold rushes in the Kalgoorlie and Murchison regions. The effects of European settlement on Aboriginal languages vary from a gradual decline in use over a number of generations, to rapid and complete extinction.

Knowledge of the Nyungar language of the southwest corner of the state has been gradually declining for 150 years. Today, younger Nyungar people may know little more than a few hundred words and a handful of phrases. These are used to replace English words in what is otherwise a variety of Aboriginal English. The original dialect diversity of Nyungar has been compromised, with

Aboriginal languages of Western Australia

Timor Sea

Kwini
Wunambal   Miriwoong
        Ngarinyin
      Worrorra
    Bardi   Gooniyandi
  Nyigina   Kija
Broome   Jaru
    Yawuru
            Kimberley
            Watmajarri

INDIAN
OCEAN
                Great Sandy Desert
        Nyangmarta   NORTHERN
Port   TERRITORY
Hedland   Yulparija
    Nyamal
              Nyiyaparli   Pintupi
Ngarluma
    Yindjibarndi   Gibson
        Banjima   Desert
Thalanyji
    Tharrkari   WESTERN
              AUSTRALIA
Yingkarta
        Pilbara
                        Great
                        Victoria
        Wajarri   Desert   SOUTH
                    Ngaanyatjarra AUSTRALIA

Nhanta
        Kalgoorlie-
        Boulder   Nullarbor Plain
        Wangkatja   Great
Perth   Australian
                              Bight
    Nyungar

500 km
250 miles

Language locations approximate only.

virtually nothing remaining of the Perth dialect, and most people using words of the eastern Nyungar areas.

English has also had an influence on the sound system and grammatical structure of modern Nyungar. The initial nasal sounds **ng** and **ny** are not used by younger speakers, who pronounce words like **nguup** (blood) as **nuup**, and Nyungar itself is now called 'Noongar'. Younger speakers also use word order to distinguish the subject and object, rather than using the case-marking system of traditional Nyungar.

Language loss in other areas has been more catastrophic. Most of the languages originally spoken along the Ashburton River are now extinct, not because their speakers have shifted more and more to English, but because whole communities were destroyed as a result of European settlement.

In some places, as elsewhere in Australia, speakers of different languages were thrown together in organised settlements. Languages were then lost as people shifted to one or two main languages away from their mother tongues. Yindjibarndi is the most successful survivor of the many languages which came together in Roebourne. As in other parts of northern Australia, a new language (called Kriol) arose in parts of the Kimberley using words borrowed mainly from English, but with a sound system and some aspects of grammar taken from traditional languages.

Western Australia today

In recent years, many Western Australian communities have increased efforts to maintain their languages and, in some cases, to revive languages which have been lost. An important part of this effort has been the establishment of community language centres that provide general language resource materials. The language centres encourage the interest of members of the general public and welcome visitors. Language centres are located in Perth, Kalgoorlie, Bunbury, Geraldton, Northam, Port Hedland, Halls Creek and Kununurra.

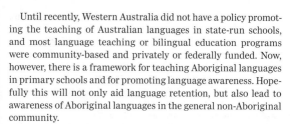

Until recently, Western Australia did not have a policy promoting the teaching of Australian languages in state-run schools, and most language teaching or bilingual education programs were community-based and privately or federally funded. Now, however, there is a framework for teaching Aboriginal languages in primary schools and for promoting language awareness. Hopefully this will not only aid language retention, but also lead to awareness of Aboriginal languages in the general non-Aboriginal community.

Language maintenance and revival is closely tied to cultural maintenance and revival, so an important aspect of this is sustaining a spiritual connection to the land. In recent times, communities have sought increased control over their traditional lands. In some areas people have moved back to their homelands and established out-stations; in other places Aboriginal community groups hold pastoral leases and so retain access to their land for traditional purposes alongside the land being used to run stock. Aboriginal rangers are increasingly involved in the management of national parks, and many communities continue to seek their rights to Native Title under federal and state law.

The Southwest

A single language, Nyungar, was spoken in the southwest of the state and existed in a number of different dialects. In the early days of contact with Europeans, a large number of loanwords were taken into English. However, the effects of European settlement then caused a catastrophic loss of language (and culture), and there are now very few fluent speakers of Nyungar remaining.

The legacy of the Nyungar people is clearest to visitors in the host of local names for places, plants and animals found in the southwest. Aboriginal heritage trails giving details of the uses of various plants, the habits of animals and historical and mythological information can be found in most national parks throughout the area.

The Murchison & Gascoyne

The main surviving language of this region is Wajarri, originally spoken in the Eastern Murchison. Although there were a number of different languages spoken in this area, the people all refer to themselves as Yamaji and will say that they speak the Yamaji language. Wajarri is also spoken in Carnarvon, where the original languages are essentially moribund. The eastern Wajarri people live in the Western Desert cultural area.

Pilbara

The southern and western Pilbara region, from the Gascoyne to the Ashburton River, formed a cultural area with the languages spoken along the Pilbara coast. The languages of this region also had similarities but, sadly, few speakers remain. A number of languages are still spoken in the northern and eastern Pilbara, the most widely known being Yindjibarndi, spoken in Roebourne, Onslow and other Pilbara towns.

The Pilbara people form a cultural group sharing similar kinship systems and ritual practices. People travel from Carnarvon in the south to Jigalong in the east and La Grange mission in the north for summer ceremonies.

Karijini, (formerly Hamersley Range National Park) is located in Panyjima, Kurrama and Yinhawangka country, while the Millstream/Chichester Ranges National Park is Kurrama and Yindjibarndi country. Aboriginal rangers from these local groups work in the parks, while local Aboriginal groups organise wilderness tours of Karijini, led by local experts.

Western Desert

Dialects of the Western Desert language are spoken across large parts of inland Western Australia and adjacent parts of South Australia and the Northern Territory. In Western Australia this language extends from near the Great Australian Bight, north to the Kimberley and west to the Hamersley Range and Murchison goldfields.

Kimberley

There were originally about 15 different prefixing languages spoken in the Kimberley region. There are marked differences in vocabulary between most of these, and they are classified as belonging to eight different language families. The languages of the remaining areas of Western Australia all belong to the Pama-Nyungan family.

Broome has speakers of Yawuru and probably also Karajarri, a Western Desert language. Cape Leveque has a population of the seagoing Bardi people. The Gibb River Road passes mainly through Ngarinyin country, and the Bungle Bungle National Park, south of Turkey Creek, has Kija and Jaru speakers. Miriwoong is spoken further to the north, around Kununurra and Lake Argyle on the Ord River.

EAST & SOUTH

The southeast of Australia, comprising the present-day areas of Victoria, Tasmania, New South Wales and the Australian Capital Territory (ACT), was settled early and intensively. When the British invaders and their descendants spread across the country, the original inhabitants were dispossessed of their land and killed in large numbers through battle, the spread of disease, and the destruction of their environment and means of living. People were also herded onto missions and government settlements, sometimes being forced to live with their enemies, and their traditional ways of life were prohibited. As a result, there was only partial transmission of traditional Aboriginal culture and language from one generation to the next, and a great deal of knowledge was lost.

Today, in New South Wales, a few old fluent speakers remain for a small number of languages, including Bundjalung of the north coast around Lismore, and Baagandji, spoken on the Darling River near Wilcannia. There are no living full speakers of a Victorian Aboriginal language, and none of the Victorian languages is used as the main means of communication in any community. However, many Aboriginal people carefully preserve some elements of their linguistic heritage, even generations after the last fluent speakers have passed away. Today, words from traditional languages can still be heard in Melbourne and Sydney, and in country areas of New South Wales and Victoria. In many communities there's rising interest in traditional languages and culture, and efforts are under way to preserve and maintain the knowledge that remains, and to augment it from written sources.

Visitors to the southeastern states will see evidence of traditional Aboriginal languages in three areas:

▶ the continuing use of Aboriginal words and expressions by Aboriginal people

▶ names for places and features of the landscape

▶ Aboriginal words that have entered the English language and are in common use by all Australians.

Aboriginal languages of Victoria, New South Wales and ACT

QUEENSLAND

SOUTH AUSTRALIA

Bundjalung

Gamilaraay

Gumbaynggir

Baagandji

NEW SOUTH WALES

Ngiyambaa

Great Dividing Range

Dharuk ○ Sydney

Wemba
Wemba

Wiradjuri

★ Canberra
ACT

VICTORIA

Yorta Yorta

Thagung-
wurrung

Watha-
wurrung ○

Woiwurrung

○ Melbourne

**TASMAN
SEA**

Warrnambool

Muk Thang

King
Island

Bass Strait

Flinders
Island

Ⓝ 0 ————— 250 km
    0 ————— 125 miles

Language locations approximate only.

WA

NT

QLD

SA

NSW

VIC

TAS

Victoria

The language that covered the area north from Melbourne almost to Echuca on the Murray River is known as Woiwurrung (for the dialect south of the Great Dividing Range) or Thagungwurrung (for the northern dialect). Other important languages of Victoria include Wathawurrung, spoken near Geelong, Wemba Wemba of northwestern Victoria, the Warrnambool language from southwestern Victoria, Yorta Yorta around the Murray east of Echuca, and Muk Thang, the language of the Ganai (also spelled Kurnai) of Gippsland.

Melbourne was first settled by Europeans in 1835, and within a few years the Aboriginal population was largely destroyed. From 1863 the survivors were placed in a reserve at Coranderrk, near Healesville, and later at other reserves such as Lake Tyers in Gippsland and Framlingham near Warrnambool in the Western District. In the 1960s, linguist Luise Hercus carried out an extensive survey of the whole state to record what could be gleaned of the traditional languages – the result was a book containing outline descriptions of three languages from northwestern Victoria and adjacent areas of New South Wales, plus word lists for a number of other languages. For most of the state our knowledge comes from word lists and very brief notes on language structures recorded by settlers, administrators and missionaries in the late 19th century.

In general, Aboriginal words tend to end in vowels, but a feature of Victorian languages is the use of a wide variety of consonants at the end of words. This is reflected in some of the plant names borrowed into English from Victorian languages, such as **ballart** (native cherry) and **murrnong** or **myrnong** (yam-daisy), and in the names of places such as **Koo-wee-rup** and **Gariwerd**. (The latter is an Aboriginal name that's been reintroduced as an alternative name for the Grampians, a mountain range in western Victoria.) For many place names it's impossible to give an exact meaning because of the lack of reliable information; however, following are some names for which the meaning is clear:

Allambee	mishearing of **ngalambi** 'to remain, dwell' – town near Yarragon, Gippsland, and Yallambie, a suburb of Melbourne
Boort	'smoke' – town in Mallee, northwestern Victoria
Coranderrk	Victorian 'Christmas bush', a small flowering tree – place near Healesville
Geelong	'tongue' – town to the west of Melbourne
Korrumburra	'march fly' – town in Gippsland
Lara	'stone' – town north of Geelong
Leongatha	'our teeth' – town in Gippsland
Mirboo	'kidney' – town in Gippsland
Narre Warren	'red' – suburb southeast of Melbourne
Wollert	'possum' – place north of Melbourne
Wonthaggi	'Fetch!' – town on the Gippsland coast

The following are some other words in Victorian languages that have entered the English language: **bunyip** (a mythical swamp-dwelling creature), **yabby** (a crustacean), **cumbungi** (bulrush), **dillon bush** (a plant), **lerp** (a form of scale), **lowan** (mallee fowl) and **tuan** (gliding possum).

Tasmania

The British takeover of Tasmania began in 1803 and most of the indigenous population was wiped out within 50 years or so. There were about a dozen Tasmanian languages and it is interesting to note that there are no clear resemblances between Tasmanian languages and those of the mainland.

No full speakers survived into the 20th century, but partial knowledge lingered on, and along with written sources this is providing the basis for teaching Palawa Kani – meaning 'Tassie blackfellas talk' – to Aboriginal children in schools. Unfortunately, records of Tasmania's languages consist almost entirely of word lists. These have been collected and published by NJB Plomley as *A Word-List of the Tasmanian Aboriginal Languages*.

New South Wales

Current knowledge of the traditional languages of New South Wales is much richer than knowledge of the languages in Victoria and Tasmania. Around Sydney and the central coast, which was settled by Europeans from 1788, the only available information is from 18th- and 19th-century records, mainly short word lists. However, for a number of other languages, especially those of inland New South Wales and the north coast, there are tape recordings, grammars and dictionaries compiled by linguists who worked with the last generation of fluent speakers.

Languages for which there's a great deal of reliable information available include Bundjalung and Gumbaynggir on the north coast; Gamilaraay (also spelled Kamilaroi), Ngiyambaa (or Wangaaybuwan) and Wiradjuri in inland New South Wales; and Baagandji (or Paakantyi) in the far west. Speakers of some of these languages remain and there are efforts under way in Aboriginal communities to revive and preserve linguistic and cultural heritage.

Throughout New South Wales, as in Victoria, there are numerous place names that have an Aboriginal origin. It's possible to give the literal translation for many of these (although information on the significance of these names in the mythology and culture is often not available). Here are some examples giving the original pronunciation and meaning:

Boggabilla	'bagaaybila'	place full of creeks
Bundarra	'bundaarra'	place of kangaroos
Cobar	'gubarr'	red ochre
Coonamble	'gunambil'	full of excrement
Gunnedah	'gunithaa'	orphan
Nambucca	'bagabaga'	knees
Torrowotto	'thuru-katu'	snake's windbreak
Uralla	'urala'	camp
Wagga Wagga	'waagan-waagan'	crows
Woolgoolga	'wiigulga'	black fig tree

Dozens of words from New South Wales languages are now part of general Australian English, especially the names of plants and animals that were new to the first European settlers. These include:

animals	**dingo; koala; wallaby; wallaroo**
artefacts	**coolamon (bark dish); gunyah (shelter); nulla-nulla (club); woomera (spear thrower)**
birds	**brolga; budgerigar; currawong; galah; kookaburra**
landscape	**billabong (river pool); gibber (stone)**
plants	**bindi-eye; coolibah; gidgee; mulga**

QUEENSLAND

The first British settlement in Queensland was a penal colony established at Moreton Bay in 1824 and moved to the site of Brisbane in 1825. By the end of the 19th century European settlers had taken over the whole of Queensland. Those Aboriginal people who were not killed in frontier battles were unable to continue their traditional way of life, and were forced to accept work, largely unpaid, on rural properties. Under the Protection Act of 1897, any Aboriginal person could be declared a ward of the state, and people were forcibly interned on reserves, sometimes in places remote from their country and people, such as Palm Island.

Queensland today

Present-day Aboriginal people in Queensland often refer to themselves as **murries** – **murry** is the word for 'man' in many of the languages of southern Queensland (including Bidjara and Biri – see the map on p212). In Brisbane there is the Murri Court, a Magistrates Court which is responsible for sentencing Aboriginal offenders. This court has Murri elders as advisers and takes into account cultural issues when determining appropriate penalties.

Given that Aboriginal people were unable to retain their traditional way of life, it's not surprising that by the middle of the 20th century there were scores of Queensland languages of which only a few elderly speakers had a full knowledge. However, languages do not die suddenly, and the last full speakers were succeeded by a generation of people with at least some knowledge of the language. Among the present generation there has been a resurgence of interest in language, and currently strenuous efforts are being made by many communities to preserve their language where some knowledge remains or to restore it from written materials.

Aboriginal languages of Queensland

Thursday Is
Cape York

PAPUA
NEW GUINEA

Weipa

Groote
Eylandt
Gulf of
Carpentaria

Wik
Cape York
Peninsula

CORAL SEA
ISLANDS
TERRITORY

Koko Pera
Mornington
Lardil Is

Guugu
Yimidhirr
Cooktown

Kuku
Yalanji
Port Douglas
Cairns

Dyirbal

Hinchinbrook Is

Townsville

CORAL
SEA

Great Barrier Reef

NORTHERN TERRITORY

Kalkadoon
Mt Isa

QUEENSLAND

Whitsunday Is

Biri
Mackay

Pitta-Pitta
Boulia

Longreach

Great Dividing Range

Emerald

Rockhampton
Curtis Island
Gladstone

Simpson
Desert

Bidjara

Bundaberg
Hervey Bay
Fraser Is
Maryborough

Charleville

Margany
Gunya

Gabi-Gabi

SOUTH
AUSTRALIA

Wangkumara

Gunggari
Toowoomba

Brisbane

NEW SOUTH WALES

Bundjalung

Yagara

Language locations approximate only.

WA   NT   QLD
      SA   NSW
            VIC
            TAS

Cape York

In Cape York there was less European intrusion, and traditional life and languages have been better maintained. Languages that have survived in the Cape York area include Koko Pera (also spelt 'Berra') on the west coast of the peninsula south of the Mitchell River, and the Wik languages of the Aurukun area further to the north. Kuku Yalanji, a language of the Bloomfield River area south of Cooktown, is still spoken. Guugu Yimidhirr (also spelt 'Guugu Yimithirr'), the language of the area just to the north of Cooktown, is still spoken, but the language of younger speakers is somewhat modified and influenced by English. This is a common phenomenon. **Koko**, **Kuku** and **Guugu** are, by the way, different spellings of the same word, which means 'language'.

The Yimidhirr people have a particular claim to fame – they gave the word **kangaroo** to English and ultimately to other languages. The Yimidhirr first encountered Europeans when Captain Cook beached the *Endeavour* for repairs in 1770. Members of Cook's party elicited some vocabulary including **kangaroo**. Later some doubt was cast on the authenticity of this word, but it is definitely a Guugu Yimidhirr word. The form is actually **kang-u-rru**, with the **ng** pronounced as in 'singer', not as in 'finger'.

The Yagara language of the Brisbane area has also provided Australian English with a number of words, including several that are not easily recognisable as Aboriginal words. These include **dilly** (as in 'dilly bag'), **bung** (in 'go bung', meaning 'cease to function'), **yakka** 'hard work' and **humpy** 'hut', though the last of these has been distorted somewhat from the original, which is **ngumpi**.

SOUTH AUSTRALIA

The first official British settlement in South Australia was established on the site of Adelaide in 1836, though whalers and sealers had been living on Kangaroo Island since the early 1800s and kidnapping Aboriginal women to live with them. European settlement had spread over the whole state by the 1870s, though only sparsely in the dry north and west of the state. However, the establishment of stock routes, the Overland Telegraph and railways brought Europeans into even these remote areas, which otherwise might have escaped significant European contact. As in other parts of Australia, Aboriginal people were killed in punitive expeditions and fell prey to introduced diseases; many of the survivors were herded into missions.

Languages

As might be expected, the survival of Aboriginal people and their languages in South Australia largely relates to the intensity of white settlement. In the southeast corner of the state, the Buandik (or Bunganditj) people were driven to near extinction and their language is known only from early records. In contrast, dialects of the Western Desert language are still spoken in the far northwest of the state, including Pitjantjatjara and Yankutjatjara. Kukata, a more southerly language, no longer has full speakers. In between these extremes there are a score of languages that have ceased to be in regular use. The Kaurna people of the Adelaide Plains were the first to lose their lands to the intruders, though the language survived into the early 20th century. The Ngarrindjeri people living around the mouth of the Murray retained their language, Yaralde, up to the 1950s.

FLINDERS RANGES DREAMING

The 'spirit of place', almost palpable in the Flinders Ranges, has inspired a rich heritage of Dreaming stories. Many of these are secret, but others related by Adnyamathanha Elders explain the creation of the landscape and the native birds and animals that inhabit it.

Arkaroola comes from Arkaroo, the name of the Dreaming Serpent Ancestor. Suffering from a powerful thirst, Arkaroo drank Lake Frome dry, then dragged his bloated body back into the ranges, carving out the sinuous Arkaroola Creek as he went. He went underground to sleep, but all that salty water gave him a belly ache. Now he constantly moves about to relieve the pain – the reason for the 30 to 40 small earth tremors that occur in the area every year.

Another story relates that the walls of Ikara (Wilpena Pound) are the bodies of two Akurra (giant snakes), who coiled around Ikara during an initiation ceremony, creating a whirlwind during which they devoured most of the participants.

There's also a story that explains why crows are black: the bossy eagle Wildu sought revenge on his nephews, who had tried to kill him by building a great fire. All the birds were caught in the flames, and, originally white, they emerged blackened and burnt. The magpies and willy wagtails were partially scorched, but the crows were entirely blackened, and have remained so to this day.

Further north and west are a number of languages that have lost their last full speakers over the last few decades. These include Diyari, Arabana, and Wirangu.

Aboriginal languages of South Australia

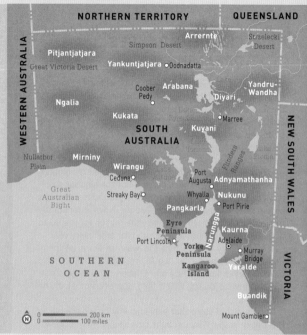

NORTHERN TERRITORY

QUEENSLAND

WESTERN AUSTRALIA

Arrernte

Simpson Desert

Strzelecki Desert

Pitjantjatjara

Great Victoria Desert

Yankuntjatjara ○ Oodnadatta

Coober Pedy ○

Arabana

Diyari

Yandru-Wandha

Ngalia

Kukata

SOUTH AUSTRALIA

Marree ●

Kuyani

NEW SOUTH WALES

Nullarbor Plain

Mirniny

Wirangu

Flinders Ranges

Ceduna ○

Port Augusta

Adnyamathanha

Great Australian Bight

Streaky Bay ○

Whyalla ●

Nukunu

Port Pirie ●

Pangkarla

Eyre Peninsula

Port Lincoln ○

Yorke Peninsula

Narunga

Kaurna

Adelaide ○

Murray Bridge ●

VICTORIA

SOUTHERN OCEAN

Kangaroo Island

Yaralde

Buandik

Mount Gambier ○

0 ___ 200 km
0 ___ 100 miles

Language locations approximate only.

WA
NT
QLD
SA
NSW
VIC
TAS

South Australia today

Today, across most of South Australia Aboriginal people speak various forms of Aboriginal English. In the area around Adelaide and to the south this is called 'Nunga English' – **nunga** is a word for 'Aborigine' taken from the Streaky Bay area. The vocabulary is mainly from English, but includes some Aboriginal words such as **bandabri** 'gun' and **kappa** 'tobacco' from Kaurna, and **marra** 'hand' and **guna** 'faeces', which are found in a large number of Australian languages.

At present, as in other areas, there is a strong move to maintain Aboriginal languages that are still living and to restore and reclaim those that are no longer in regular use. The Kaurna people, for instance, have a strong sense of identity and are now attempting to revive their language on the basis of early records.

INDIGENOUS LANGUAGES

TORRES STRAIT

There are three Torres Strait Islander languages, and they're spoken by a population that is of largely Melanesian, but also European, Asian and Aboriginal, background. Their home-lands are a group of small islands scattered along the waterway known as Torres Strait, between the tip of Cape York and Papua New Guinea (see the map opposite).

There are about 30,000 Torres Strait Islanders, but only about 6000 still live in the Torres Strait. The remaining 80% have moved to towns and cities in the mainland of Australia for various reasons – mainly for jobs, good health and better edu-cation for their children. Most Torres Strait Islanders who have decided to move to the mainland have settled in the coastal towns and cities of Queensland.

···

Languages

Two of the Torres Strait Islander languages are original indig-enous languages. Kala Lagaw Ya (KLY) is spoken by the people of the western islands of Saibai (and thus now in Seisia and Bamaga), Dauan, Boigu, Mabuiag, Muralag, Badu, Moa (Kubin) and Narupai, and the central islands of Masig, Purma, Yam and Warraber. Meriam Mir (MM) is spoken by the people from the eastern islands of Mer (where it is primarily spoken by adults), Erub and Ugar. Kala Lagaw Ya is believed to be related to Aus-tralian Aboriginal languages. Meriam Mir, on the other hand, belongs to the Trans Fly family of languages along the Papuan coast.

The third indigenous language of Torres Strait Islanders is an English-based creole called Torres Strait Broken (TSB). It's an established lingua franca, mainly spoken in the eastern and central Islands and Thursday Island, and is the first language

Torres Strait
inhabited islands & linguistic boundaries

PAPUA
NEW GUINEA

Daru
Island

Boigu
Island

Dauan
Island

Saibai
Island

Ugar
(Stephen Island)

Erub
(Darnley Island)

T o r r e s   S t r a i t

Meriam Mir

Kala Lagaw Ya

Masig
(Yorke Island)

Mer
(Murray Island)

Mabuiag
(Jervis Island)

Yam Island

Badu
(Mulgrave Island)

Badu

St Pauls

Purma
(Coconut Island)

Kubin

Moa
(Banks Island)

Warraber
(Sue Island)

Kiriri
(Hammond
Island)

Waiben
(Thursday
Island)

**C O R A L
S E A**

Narupai
(Horn Island)

Muralag
(Prince of
Wales Island)

Seisia

Great Barrier Reef

Bamaga

Cape York Peninsula

QUEENSLAND

AUSTRALIA

N

0 — — — — — — 50 km
0 — — — — — — 25 miles

Kala Lagaw Ya — — dialect

Meriam Mir - - - - borders

Language locations approximate only.

WA

NT

SA

QLD

NSW

VIC

TAS

of most people there who were born after World War II. Nevertheless, most adults also maintain their traditional languages.

Thursday Island has a mixed community of European, Asian and Aboriginal people. English is an official language and is used extensively in government offices, schools, churches, hospitals, shops and so on. The two indigenous languages are often used by their speakers among themselves, but Torres Strait Broken, as mentioned, is the most commonly used language on the island.

Despite exposure to the dominant western culture and English language, Torres Strait Islanders on the mainland have managed to maintain their traditional languages exceptionally well, with the help of various programs. (Details are available from the Federation of Aboriginal and Torres Strait Islander Languages at www.fatsil.org.) Kala Lagaw Ya has about 3000 speakers, while there are around 2000 Meriam Mir speakers, and all Torres Strait Islanders speak Torres Strait Broken, regardless of where they live in Australia.

European influence

European contact has had devastating effects on the Torres Strait languages and culture. The colonisation process and cruel policies of assimilation, segregation and integration have greatly contributed to the marginalisation of Torres Strait Islander culture and languages. There were official limitations on the use of indigenous languages in schools and public places.

The creation of Torres Strait Broken was one result of colonisation. It was developed mainly from the Pacific Island pidgin called Bislama, which was brought to Torres Strait by Pacific Islanders working in the area's marine industry. Other migrant groups, such as Japanese, Malays and Chinese, also had an influence, and Torres Strait Broken is now distinctly different from Bislama.

Community & cultural life

The fundamental aspects of the original Torres Strait Islander culture have remained intact, despite colonisation. However, since the time of initial contact, some aspects have changed, both as a result of the dominance of European culture and the influence of other cultures that the Islanders have come into contact with. Nevertheless, Torres Strait Islanders are still able to practise elements of their traditional way of life.

The most notable cultural practice that Torres Strait Islanders on all islands have hung on to, apart from their languages, is traditional dance. There are a number of styles of traditional dance, which can be performed either while standing upright and stamping both feet or while in a sitting position. Both forms of dancing require a lot of hand movements and jumping. The dancers usually wear special costumes, depending on what the dance is about – men wear a piece of cloth called **lava-lava** and a singlet, while women wear specially made floral dresses. The dancers also equip themselves with special regalia consisting of grass-skirt, headdress, headbands, necklaces, arm and leg bands and models representing the subject that the dance portrays. All dances are usually accompanied by singing and drumming.

Over the years, Torres Strait Islanders developed a lifestyle suited to their environment. At one time they depended almost entirely on the sea for food and for transport from one island to the next. On land, they both cultivated crops in their gardens and domesticated animals, mainly pigs. These days not much gardening is being carried out – Torres Strait Islanders rely more and more on community grocery stores. Fish is still the staple food, however, caught by handlines and nets or hand spears. It's supplemented with rice, yams, sweet potatoes and taro. Other important sources of seafood are dugong and turtle, which are hunted in the traditional way with a special harpoon. (Both dugong and turtle are considered a luxury, and are only eaten on special occasions like weddings and tombstone unveilings.)

The outer island communities are changing fairly rapidly from traditional villages to small townships. All the islands now have modern houses, schools, medical facilities, telephones and electricity. However, in general, life on the islands proceeds at a notably leisurely pace. The daily activities of the people revolve around family and community affairs.

Torres Strait Islanders are devout Christians, and most belong to the Anglican church, though some islands have smaller churches of other denominations. Church services are normally conducted in English but most of the hymns are sung in the indigenous languages.

Dialects

Kala Lagaw Ya

Kala Lagaw Ya (KLY) is a language with four dialects:

- the Kala Kawaw Ya (KKY) of the islands of Saibai, Dauan and Boigu
- Mabuiag (M) of Mabuiag Island and Badu
- Kaurareg (K) of Kubin (Moa)
- Nurapai (Horn Island).

The differences between these dialects are minimal and lie mainly in words and sounds.

Meriam Mir

Meriam Mir (MM) had two dialects and the differences between them were restricted to words and sounds. Sadly, only the Mer dialect has survived.

Torres Strait Broken

As in the Kriol spoken in the Top End, the vocabulary of Torres Strait Broken varies quite widely, with different words being derived from the indigenous languages in the eastern and central/western islands. For example:

Awa, yumi go.   Uncle, let's go. (eastern)

Awadhe, yumi go.   Uncle, let's go. (central/western)

....

Greetings & civilities

Kala Lagaw Ya

How are you?	**Ngi midh?** (KKY)
	Ni midhikidh? (M & K)
Fine.	**Balabayginga.** (KKY)
	Matha mina. (M & K)
Have you eaten?	**Ngi aydu purathima a?** (KKY)
	Ni aydun purthema a? (M)
	Ni aydun purthema? (K)
I've eaten already.	**Ngath aygud mu-asin.** (KKY)
	Ngaw/Nguzu aygud mina-asin. m/f (M & K)
I haven't eaten yet.	**Ngay aydu purthayginga.** (KKY)
	Ngaw/Nguzu ayngu purthayginga. m/f (M & K)
Come inside the house!	**Aya, ngapa lagiya muyari!** (KKY)
	Aye, ngapa mudhiya uth! (M & K)
Thank you.	**Eso.** (KKY, M & K)
Very good.	**Mina boelbayginga.** (KKY)
	Matha mina. (M & K)

INDIGENOUS LANGUAGES

Meriam Mir

How are you?	**Nako manali?**
Fine.	**Sikakanali.**
Have you eaten?	**Aka ma lewer erwe?**
I've eaten already.	**Kai emethu lewer erwe.**
I haven't eaten yet.	**Ka nole lewer erwe.**
Come inside the house!	**Ma thaba bau mithem!**
Thank you.	**Eswau.**
Very good.	**Dhebe kaine.**

Torres Strait Broken

How are you?	**Wis wei (yu)?**
Fine.	**Orait.**
Have you eaten?	**U bi kaikai?**
I've eaten already.	**Ai bi pinis kaikai.**
I haven't eaten yet.	**Ai no bi kaikai.**
Come inside the house!	**Kam insaid hous!**
Thank you.	**Eso po yu.**
Very good.	**Prapa gud.**

Notes

Wordfinder

Index

W

Look out for these...

> **CHARGE LIKE A WOUNDED BULL**
> — CHARGE OUTRAGEOUSLY HIGH PRICES

> **CHUCK A BERKO**
> — EXPRESS EXTREME ANGER; LOSE YOUR TEMPER

> **HAVE A FEW KANGAROOS LOOSE IN THE TOP PADDOCK**
> — CRAZY

> **RUNNING AROUND LIKE A HEADLESS CHOOK**
> — MAKING A LOT OF COMMOTION BUT GETTING NOWHERE

> **FLAT OUT LIKE A LIZARD DRINKING**
> — VERY BUSY